All too often, I visit homes in which the father figure is not a part of the family unit and the family is dysfunctional. Having had a father with a very strong commitment to the love and safety of his family, I am grateful every day for being raised in an environment that helped shape the type of person I am today. I feel it is my responsibility to raise my children in the same loving and supportive manner. *The Warrior Within* is a must-read for fathers in today's society. It is truly an inspiration.

TOMMY BOWDEN
HEAD FOOTBALL COACH, CLEMSON UNIVERSITY

Through Asher, a little-known Old Testament patriarch, Pat Williams challenges the men of today to step up to the plate with their families. *The Warrior Within* will stir you to examine your role in your family and challenge you to become a complete and godly man like Asher.

VAN CHANCELLOR
HEAD COACH, WNBA HOUSTON COMETS

Who knew that such a precious nugget lay buried in the Old Testament genealogies? Pat Williams mines a segment of Scripture that most people skip over and discovers a wealth of advice for men, fathers and husbands. I wish I had the benefit of this book when I was raising my own kids. I'm making sure that they have the benefit of it as they lead their own families.

MIKE HUCKABEE
GOVERNOR OF ARKANSAS

Some works prove timeless. *The Warrior Within* is a resource for generations. Fathers will hand it down to their sons.

BILL MCCARTNEY
FOUNDER, PROMISE KEEPERS
FORMER HEAD FOOTBALL COACH, UNIVERSITY OF COLORADO

The Warrior Within should be required reading for every man in America. You'll learn about four principles that will radically transform every area of your life. Plunge in and thank me later.

DAN REEVES
FOOTBALL OPERATIONS EXECUTIVE, HOUSTON TEXANS

Pat Williams has discovered a treasure in one of the Bible genealogies! Way to go! Learn from Asher how to be a brave warrior and man of integrity as well as a godly husband and father. Apply what you have learned for your family and share it with your men's group!

BOB RUSSELL
SENIOR MINISTER, SOUTHEAST CHRISTIAN CHURCH
LOUISVILLE, KENTUCKY

The Warrior Within shows us the way with the kind of transparency that endears and empowers us to lead successfully! An utterly fascinating read!

SPENCER TILLMAN
LEAD STUDIO ANALYST, CBS SPORTS
AUTHOR, *SCORING IN THE RED ZONE*

There is no one better equipped or qualified to challenge, motivate and inspire men than Pat Williams. His track record speaks for itself. Pat is a modern-day Asher, who models manhood God's way—in fatherhood, character, boldness and leadership. I recommend *The Warrior Within* to any man who yearns to impact this world for God and leave a legacy that counts for the Kingdom.

ED YOUNG
PASTOR, SECOND BAPTIST CHURCH
HOUSTON, TEXAS

THE
WARRIOR
WITHIN

PAT WILLIAMS
with JIM DENNEY

Regal

From Gospel Light
Ventura, California, U.S.A.

PUBLISHED BY REGAL BOOKS
FROM GOSPEL LIGHT
VENTURA, CALIFORNIA, U.S.A.

Regal PRINTED IN THE U.S.A.

Regal Books is a ministry of Gospel Light, a Christian publisher dedicated to serving the local church. We believe God's vision for Gospel Light is to provide church leaders with biblical, user-friendly materials that will help them evangelize, disciple and minister to children, youth and families.

It is our prayer that this Regal book will help you discover biblical truth for your own life and help you meet the needs of others. May God richly bless you.

For a free catalog of resources from Regal Books/Gospel Light, please call your Christian supplier or contact us at 1-800-4-GOSPEL or www.regalbooks.com.

Library of Congress Cataloging-in-Publication Data
Williams, Pat, 1940-
  The warrior within / Pat Williams with Jim Denney.
    p. cm.
  ISBN 0-8307-3902-5 (hard cover)
  1. Men (Christian theology) 2. Men—Religious life. I. Denney, James D. II. Title.

BT703.5.W55 2006   2005035898
248.8'42—dc22

1   2   3   4   5   6   7   8   9   10   /   10   09   08   07   06

Rights for publishing this book in other languages are contracted by Gospel Light Worldwide, the international nonprofit ministry of Gospel Light. Gospel Light Worldwide also provides publishing and technical assistance to international publishers dedicated to producing Sunday School and Vacation Bible School curricula and books in the languages of the world. For additional information, visit www.gospellightworldwide.org; write to Gospel Light Worldwide, P.O. Box 3875, Ventura, CA 93006; or send an e-mail to info@gospellightworldwide.org.

This book is gratefully
dedicated to Pastor Cal Rychener,
a choice man of God,
a warrior and a leader.
If not for you, Cal, this book
would not have happened.
Thank you, my friend.

ASHER AND HIS FAMILY

The sons of Asher:

 Imnah, Ishvah, Ishvi and Beriah. Their sister was Serah.

The sons of Beriah:

 Heber and Malkiel, who was the father of Birzaith.

Heber was the father of Japhlet, Shomer and Hotham and of their sister Shua.

The sons of Japhlet:

 Pasach, Bimhal and Ashvath.

 These were Japhlet's sons.

The sons of Shomer:

 Ahi, Rohgah, Hubbah and Aram.

The sons of his brother Helem:

 Zophah, Imna, Shelesh and Amal.

The sons of Zophah:

 Suah, Harnepher, Shual, Beri, Imrah, Bezer, Hod, Shamma, Shilshah, Ithran and Beera.

The sons of Jether:

 Jephunneh, Pispah and Ara.

The sons of Ulla:

 Arah, Hanniel and Rizia.

All these were descendents of Asher—heads of families, choice men, brave warriors and outstanding leaders. The number of men ready for battle, as listed in their genealogy, was 26,000.

       —1 Chronicles 7:30-40

CONTENTS

Ready for Battle

Mike Singletary

*NFL Hall of Fame linebacker (inducted 1998), ten-time
Pro Bowl player, two-time NFL Defensive Player of the Year
(1985 and 1988), and NFL Man of the Year (1990)*

Life is a battle, and the Christian life is the most intense battle of all.
It takes a real warrior to live the Christian life, because our enemy is
playing for keeps. That's why I encourage you to read this book, *The
Warrior Within*, by Pat Williams. It's based on the life of a little-known
Old Testament hero named Asher. Frankly, I didn't know much about
Asher before reading *The Warrior Within*. But as I learned Asher's story,
I was struck by the fact that the four themes that defined his life are
truly the four great themes of my life. I'm not saying I've mastered
these principles, but I have certainly set my sights on them! Those four
principles are:

1. Be a Great Husband and a Great Dad
The eight most important people in my life are Kim (my wife) and my
seven children. I have a solemn responsibility before God to love, teach
and lead my family. My number one priority as a Christian father is to
lead my kids to know and love Jesus Christ.

I had to learn what it means to be a Christian father because godly
fatherhood was not modeled for me when I was young. My parents were
married in their teens and our home life was troubled. I was the
youngest of ten kids, and my dad, who was a preacher, left our family
and the ministry when I was 12. My mother kept the family together

with her love and prayers, but I grew up with a lot of resentment toward my absent father.

Once, at a family reunion, I looked around and realized that almost all my brothers had gone through a divorce. I heard the ex-wives talking about how hard it was not having husbands as the head of their households. I saw that the effect of my father's abandonment was being passed down to later generations. I realized I had to let Jesus free me of my resentment if I wanted to truly live as the kind of father God intended me to be.

Kim and I are committed to keeping our marriage and family strong through what we call the "Three Cs of Marriage." First C: *Communication*. We talk, we listen, we serve one another by keeping the lines of communication open. Second C: *Commitment*. We take our wedding vows seriously. Feelings go up and down, but we know that a promise-keeping commitment will carry us through the tough times. Third C: *Companionship*. Marriage should be fun. Kim and I try to renew our friendship every day.

This man Asher must have been quite a husband and father, because 1 Chronicles 7:40 tells us that *all* of his descendents were "heads of families." All of them!

2. Be a "Choice Man" of Character

Because the Christian life is a battle, we need to be choice men of character. We have to be men of honesty, courage, hard work, humility and more. We need to have our priorities squared away. We have to set an example for those who follow after us. Our kids need to see consistency and integrity in our lives.

As men of God, we have to be willing to humble ourselves and demonstrate Christlike character to others. God brought that lesson home to me one time when I visited the Cook County Women's Prison in Chicago to minister, talk about Jesus, and bring a message of hope to the women prisoners who were there. When I got to the prison, the chaplain told me not to expect much of a response. He was right. I went into the room and started talking about what the Lord had done in my life—and I got nothing in return but hard stares.

And that's when I heard God speaking to me. I heard Him say, very gently and quietly, "Mike, these women need to see you humble yourself before them." So I got down on my knees and said, "I'm kneeling here in the place of all the men who have abandoned you and hurt you and caused pain in your life. On behalf of those men, I ask your forgiveness."

Then something amazing happened. Where there had been hard stares, I now saw tears rolling down the cheeks of those women. I saw all the brokenness and pain in their lives. And the Lord began to do a healing work in their lives.

I learned the value of the character quality of humility. God taught me how important it is for a man to be willing to get on his knees and, in the spirit of Christ, ask to be forgiven.

This man Asher must have had a lot of character, because 1 Chronicles 7:40 tells us that *all* of his descendents were "choice men" of character, "choice men" of God.

3. Be a Warrior for God

Football teaches us that there are two kinds of people: warriors and spectators. Don't get me wrong—I love the fans. But the fans don't suit up, they don't line up, and they don't give and take the big hits. That's the warrior's job.

In my life, as in football, I choose to be a warrior, not a spectator. I'm a warrior against hate and ignorance, poverty and injustice. I'm a warrior for God and for the gospel of Jesus Christ. Life is warfare, and no warfare is more intense than *spiritual* warfare.

I remember what it was like to put a big bone-jarring hit on another player. It felt like a lightning strike. For a moment, there's a blast of white heat that shines through your mind and body. It hurts, it makes you see double—and it feels great! I love that feeling of being a warrior, of giving everything I've got to achieve a victory. I love the helmet-busting intensity of the game.

This man Asher must have been an intense and fierce warrior for God, because 1 Chronicles 7:40 tells us that *all* of Asher's descendents were "brave warriors." In fact, it says, "The number of men ready for battle, as listed in their genealogy, was 26,000." That's quite an army of warriors!

4. Be an Outstanding Leader

Leadership is a big thing with me. The position I played (middle linebacker) is the leader of the defense. The middle linebacker has to read the offensive sets, call the defensive formations, anticipate plays, and then, when the ball is snapped, elude blockers and lead the way in making the big hits. Throughout my football career, I was continually working on building my leadership skills.

I had the privilege of wearing the wishbone C of the Chicago Bears throughout my entire career. After we beat New England in Superbowl XX (1986), I suddenly received more media attention than I'd ever had in my life. That's when I realized that I was a leader on a much bigger stage than a football field. The Lord showed me that He had given me this gift of athletic ability for a reason: He wanted me to use it to glorify Him and draw other people into an eternal relationship with Him. He wanted me to be a leader in sharing the message of His kingdom.

Of course, my number one leadership role is in the home. I want my wife and kids to know beyond a shadow of a doubt that Jesus Christ is my Lord, my Savior, and my Leader. My first allegiance is to Him, and if I never fail Him, I will never fail my family. I keep that principle always before me as I ask God to help me be a shepherd to my family.

This man Asher must have been one of the greatest leaders in human history, because 1 Chronicles 7:40 tells us that *all* of Asher's descendents were "outstanding leaders."

That's the message of *The Warrior Within*. Pat Williams has done a powerful job of bringing this man Asher to life and showing us what it means to be complete in these four dimensions of godly manhood. He's written an inspiring, motivating, life-changing book. Take these principles to heart, put them to the test in your own life, and become the warrior God created you to be.

Life truly is a battle. *The Warrior Within* will arm you for the fight!

The Seven-Forty Club

Over Labor Day weekend 2004, I was in Peoria, Illinois, helplessly watching news reports as Hurricane Frances churned her way across Florida. A hurricane the size of Texas was headed straight for my home in Orlando—and I was stranded in central Illinois.

I had come to Peoria as a guest of Northwoods Community Church—a dynamic 3,000-member church designed around the needs of "spiritual seekers." After I spoke at the Sunday morning services, Pastor Cal Rychener drove me to the airport. Because of the hurricane, Pastor Cal accompanied me to the airline counter in case my flight was canceled and I needed a ride back to the hotel.

As we waited at the counter, he said, "Pat, if you get marooned in Peoria for a whole week, you can come with me to our Seven-Forty Club."

"Seven-Forty Club? What's that?"

"It's a group of men who meet the first Saturday of the month. We start at 7:40 in the morning and have breakfast, Bible study and prayer."

Intrigued, I asked, "Why 7:40? That's an odd time to meet."

"Well," he said, "a while back, I was having my morning devotions and reading through the genealogies in 1 Chronicles—you know, 'Japhlet begat Pasach,' and so on. Then I stumbled onto 1 Chronicles 7:40—"

"Aha!" I said. "*That's* where 7:40 came from!"

"Exactly," he said. "And when I read that verse, it was a 'Eureka!' moment. It shows that it's worth the effort to wade through those genealogies, because there are treasures just waiting to be discovered. In that verse, I discovered a wonderful statement about Asher and his descendents: 'All these were descendents of Asher—heads of families, choice men, brave warriors, and outstanding leaders. The number of men ready for battle, as listed in their genealogy, was 26,000.'"

I pulled out my Bible and read the verse for myself. "Wow!" I said. "Where has Asher been all my life? Asher had 26,000 descendents—and there wasn't a dud or a black sheep in the lot!"

As I reread that verse, I absorbed these facts: The descendants of Asher were "heads of families." In other words, they were godly husbands and fathers. And they were "choice men"—men of integrity and sterling character. They were also "brave warriors"—courageous men with strong convictions, ready to take a stand. And they were "outstanding leaders." In short, the descendants of Asher were everything I have been speaking and writing about for years!

What a discovery! And if it hadn't been for a hurricane in Florida, I probably never would have heard of Asher—and you wouldn't be reading this book right now.

THE BATTLEFIELDS OF LIFE

When God tells us in His Word that all of Asher's descendants—all of them!—became "heads of families, choice men, brave warriors and outstanding leaders," it's clear that Asher was a special man. There has to be a reason why Asher and his descendants were so complete in these four dimensions of godly manhood—fatherhood, character, boldness and leadership.

God never wastes His lessons. He speaks quite pointedly about Asher and his tribe, even though His description of Asher is compressed into a single verse of Scripture. God clearly wants us to take note of Asher and learn some important lessons from this long-ignored but vitally significant character from Old Testament history. I believe God wants all of us, as men of God, to become spiritual descendants and imitators of Asher, complete in the four dimensions of godly manhood. He wants us to build into our lives these simple but life-changing concepts I call the "Asher principles."

That's why I've written *The Warrior Within*. I've tried to make this a practical book, packed with insights you can use right now. These principles don't come from an ivory tower or a think tank. They come from the depths of God's Word, from the battlefields of my own life, and from the real-life experiences of men I've known and learned from.

Have you felt like a failure as a man, a husband and a father? So have I. Friend, I've been through career struggles, marital struggles, a divorce, and more parenting crises than you can imagine. In case you weren't aware, I'm "Dad" to 19 kids—4 birth kids, 14 by international adoption, and 1 by remarriage. So you won't get any condemnation from me about your struggles—just some "been there, done that" understanding.

In this book, you'll gain a sense of just why Asher was such a complete and godly man. Even though the Scriptures don't give us many details of Asher's life, we do know a lot about his character. He couldn't have had so many strong, godly descendants unless he exhibited these traits himself.

Interspersed among the chapters of this book are several brief fictional passages that portray Asher's life in imaginative form. Although these scenes are invented, they are consistent with what we know of Asher's life and times. I hope these fictional sections will help bring this warrior named Asher to life in your imagination.

MEN WHO INFLUENCE AND BLESS GENERATIONS

I had a life-changing encounter in Peoria, Illinois, on Labor Day weekend 2004. God took me 964 miles from home and allowed a hurricane to cross my path just to make sure I would discover the Asher principles.

And just as God didn't lead me to Peoria by accident, this book didn't end up in your hands by accident. I'm convinced that God wants you and me to understand that we each occupy a strategic place in history—in our family history, in our world's history, in God's plan for human history. Each of us is an "Asher," a human link between the past and the future. God wants us to become the kind of men who will influence and bless generations to come.

Ever since that life-changing visit to Peoria, I've been learning everything I can about Asher—a man whose godly influence extended far beyond his mortal lifetime. I've been thinking about him, studying the times and culture in which he lived, and discovering everything that can be known about him. Here's what my research has turned up:

- *His family of origin:* Asher was the eighth son of Jacob. His mother was Zilpah, the maid of one of Jacob's wives, Leah. Asher's only full brother was his older brother Gad.
- *The meaning of his name:* "Asher" means "happy." Genesis 30:13 tells us that when Zilpah, Leah's maid, gave birth, Leah said, "How happy I am! The women will call me happy." So Leah, the wife of Jacob, named the boy Asher, or "Happy." In a sense, this happy boy named Asher had two mothers to look after him, Leah and Zilpah.
- *The prophecies of Jacob and Moses:* When Jacob blessed his 12 sons in Genesis 49, he predicted, "Asher's food will be rich; he will provide delicacies fit for a king" (v. 20). In Deuteronomy 33:24-25, Moses also blessed Asher and his tribe: "Most blessed of sons is Asher; let him be favored by his brothers, and let him bathe his feet in oil. The bolts of your gates will be iron and bronze, and your strength will equal your days." Both of these prophecies were richly fulfilled in the history of Israel. The tribe of Asher possessed land that was fertile for growing olive trees, so there was always an abundance of olive oil and wealth for the descendents of Asher. In fact, the lands once possessed by the tribe of Asher are still rich olive-growing regions to this day.
- *The character of Asher:* Though Scripture tells us very little about Asher's character, Jewish rabbinical literature tells us that Asher was an honest and honorable man. According to tradition, Asher was the one son of Jacob who continually tried to settle disputes and reconcile his quarrelsome brothers. From ancient times, Asher was regarded by Jewish religious tradition as a prime example of a virtuous man who was focused on bringing peace to his family and building relationships among his brothers.
- *Quality, not quantity:* The 26,000-man tribe of Asher was not the most numerous tribe in Israel, but the descendents of Asher were "choice" men, the cream of the crop. The Asherites were known for quality, not quantity.

Asher and his descendents were men of honor, virtue, might and influence. The way they lived their lives was a blessing to the generations that followed. They didn't live for themselves or for the moment. They lived for the ages. They lived for their children, grandchildren, and even for generations of children they would never even know.

Almost a century ago, a writer named F. M. Bareham made a profound observation about the year 1809. That was the year the entire world waited for news of Napoleon's war against Austria. People thought that the history of civilization turned on whether Napoleon won or lost that war. A hundred years later, Napoleon's battlefield exploits were largely forgotten. His forces fought the Austrian army to a standstill, leaving little impact on history.

Yet there were other events that took place during 1809—events that went almost entirely unnoticed at the time, but which affect the way we live our lives today. What happened in 1809 that so altered the course of history? Babies were born! Abraham Lincoln was born in 1809. As the sixteenth president of the United States, Lincoln led the Union during the Civil War and freed the slaves. Our lives would be very different today if he had never been born. Charles Darwin was born in 1809. The British naturalist revolutionized scientific thinking with his theory of evolution by natural selection. Other great people born in 1809 included William Gladstone, the English statesman and government reformer; Oliver Wendell Holmes, Sr., the famed American physician and father of Supreme Court Justice Oliver Wendell Holmes, Jr.; the great English poet Alfred, Lord Tennyson; German composer Felix Mendelssohn; Louis Braille, inventor of the Braille writing system for the blind; and American poet and story writer Edgar Allan Poe.

F. M. Bareham concluded, "Which of the battles of 1809 mattered more than the babies of 1809?"[1] It's true. God achieves His purposes through people, and every person in the world starts life as a child.

More than 3,000 years ago, an Egyptian princess found a Hebrew baby floating in a little basket. That baby became Moses the Lawgiver, who delivered Israel from bondage. And more than 2,000 years ago, another Hebrew baby was born in a little village called Bethlehem. That child became Jesus the Savior, who died on the cross and delivered us from bondage to sin. As someone once said, when God wants to do something great in the world, He sends a child to do it.

Asher understood this principle and he lived by it. He was a complete and godly man who fully exemplified the four crucial dimensions of manhood—fatherhood, character, boldness and leadership. Through him, God brought generations of godly men into the world—men who shaped history for the better. And every one of those men started as a child.

The long-neglected legacy of Asher has been rediscovered—in Peoria, Illinois! Now that legacy has come into your town and into your life. Read on with me and learn how you can become part of Asher's spiritual legacy. Learn how you can become a godly warrior like Asher—a man who blesses children and influences generations.

Note

1. F. M. Bareham, quoted in Spencer W. Kimball, *Faith Precedes the Miracle: Based on Discourses of Spencer W. Kimball* (Deseret Book Company, 1972).

DIMENSION 1:
FATHERHOOD

IMAGINE A FATHER . . .

Asher and his four sons worked in the hillside vineyard overlooking a green valley. The muscles of Asher's arms and his chest glistened with sweat. He was tall, lean and bearded, with long black hair that flowed to his shoulders. Working with practiced skill, he pruned the vines and stripped away the overgrowth. His three eldest sons, Imnah, Ishvah and Ishvi, worked the next row. The three of them pruned as many vines in an hour as Asher pruned by himself.

"Why do we have to prune these vines?" asked 11-year-old Ishvi, Asher's third-born. He was lean and brown-skinned, and his face was always lined with thought. Asher had given each of his four sons a nickname, and he called Ishvi "The Philosopher" because Ishvi questioned everything.

"We prune the vines," Asher replied, "so that the vineyard will produce more fruit."

"How can that be?" asked Ishvi. "If you want more grapes, you should let the vine grow bigger, not cut it back."

"That's stupid," sneered 17-year-old Imnah, the eldest. He was a ruggedly-built young man with a thick neck and well-muscled arms. Asher had nicknamed him "The Chieftain" because he lorded it over his brothers.

"Hush, Imnah!" Asher admonished. "Ishvi, we prune the vines to discipline the vineyard. You have to force the vines to work harder if you want more fruit. If you don't prune the vines, they get lazy. They make too many canes, too many leaves, and not enough grapes. Do you see now?"

"I guess so," Ishvi said. "But why did you plant the vineyard on a hillside? It would be easier to work in the vineyard if the ground was level."

"The hillside has good drainage," Asher said, "and the southern exposure gives the grapes plenty of sun so they'll grow big and sweet."

"Serah's coming," said Ishvah, Asher's second-born. "She's bringing water." Ishvah was the sharp-eyed one, the son with the quick strategic mind and fearless heart. Asher had nicknamed him "The Warrior." Though barely in his teens, Ishvah was skilled with a bow and arrow, and could shoot the eye out of a sparrow at a hundred yards.

Asher shielded his eyes and scanned the valley, the house, the olive press, the stone cistern, but he didn't see Serah anywhere—

There she is! He saw the top of little Serah's head. She was near the foot of the hill, walking between two vine rows, almost completely hidden. Asher never ceased to be amazed at Ishvah's keen eyesight. The boy would be a great warrior someday.

Asher and his sons continued working in silence. They would cut the vines, move down the row, cut more vines—

"Father," said Ishvi, The Philosopher, "are we poor?"

"Of course not," Asher said. "The Lord gives us a rich harvest every season, more than enough for our needs. We have this vineyard, fig orchards to the north, olive groves to the west, and wheat fields in the valley. We are very blessed, my son."

The answer didn't seem to satisfy The Philosopher. "Father, I think we are poor," he said. "If we were rich, we wouldn't have to work so hard."

"Work is a blessing from the Lord, Ishvi," Asher said.

"But we work all the time! It never ends!" said Ishvi. "In winter, we prune the grape vines. Next month, we prune the olive trees. In spring, the grape vines must be tied and the wheat must be planted. In summer, we harvest the wheat. In fall, we harvest the grapes, figs and olives. If we must always be working, then we *must* be poor!"

"It's not work that makes a man poor," Asher said. "Only laziness can do that. Why do you bring this up, Ishvi? Did someone tell you we're poor?"

Ishvi nodded. "Arad said so."

Asher lifted one eyebrow. "Arad? The son of Elkanah the Metalsmith?"

"He says his family is rich," said Ishvi, "because his father buys silver from Tarshish and gold from Uphaz. Arad says he never has to prune vines or harvest figs because his father is rich."

"A metalsmith trades in silver and gold," Asher said. "I trade in grapes and figs, wheat and oil. The family of Elkanah is rich in some things. The family of Asher is rich in others."

Just then, Asher heard Serah's sing-song voice, high and clear. "There is no one holy like the Lord," the child sang. "There is no one besides You! There is no Rock like our God!"

Moments later, Asher saw his daughter coming along the row of freshly pruned vines. Little Serah was slender and graceful, with large brown eyes like those of a doe. Her raven-black hair and brown skin stood out against the white linen of her robe. She carried a short pole over one shoulder with a skin of water tied at each end. Her footsteps kept time with her song.

"Here comes my Angel," Asher said, using his pet name for her. He got down on one knee and set his knife on the ground, then he spread his arms wide. "Come here, little Angel! Give your Abba a hug!"

Serah dropped the water skins and ran into his arms. "Abba! Abba!"

As his arms encircled her, Serah screamed and struggled. "Eww! You're all sweaty! And you smell bad, too!"

Asher laughed and tickled her ribs. "That's the stink of good honest labor! If I didn't smell so bad, this family wouldn't eat so well!"

"I don't care! Let me go!"

Chuckling, he released her. She backed away, holding her nose, but grinning. No matter how he smelled, Serah loved her Abba—her Daddy.

Asher picked up the water skins and tossed one to his eldest son. Then he opened the other skin and drank deeply. The water was cool and clean on his tongue. It left a faint taste of cistern stone and goat leather in his mouth.

"Abba!" said a little-boy voice.

Asher looked down and saw his youngest son, Beriah, standing in his shadow, licking parched lips. Too little to wield a pruning knife, Beriah did his part by carrying away the cuttings to be heaped and burned.

"I'm thirsty, Abba!" the boy said.

Asher grinned and handed the water skin to his littlest son. "Here, young Lion," he said. "You've been working the hardest of us all. Drink the rest. You've earned it."

Beriah took the water skin from his father's hand. He drank it all down, taking care not to spill a drop.

When Asher's sons had emptied both water skins, they handed them back to Serah. Before she could escape, Asher hugged his daughter to him and planted a kiss on her cheek. Serah screamed and wriggled. "Eww! The smell! Let me go!"

Asher released her, and she picked up her pole and danced away, giggling. Taking up his pruning knife, Asher called to his sons, "Back to work, men!" Father and sons returned to their task.

After a while, Ishvah, The Warrior, broke the silence. "Father," he said, "I've heard that the Midianites have been raiding the farms around the Jezreel Valley. They say that 200 were killed at the pass near Megiddo."

"I've heard the same tales," Asher said.

"Do you think the Midianites will come to our valley?" There was no fear, only excitement, in Ishvah's voice.

"Don't be too eager for battle, my son," Asher said. "If the Midianites come here, we'll be ready. But I pray they do not come."

"I pray they do," Ishvah said.

"Why do the Midianites hate us, father?" asked Ishvi, The Philosopher.

"They hate us because we worship God Most High," said Asher. "Their gods are dead idols made of brass."

"Will we have to fight them?" asked Ishvi, a faint tremor in his voice.

Overhead, a cloud obscured the sun. The hillside darkened.

"If they come," Asher said, "my sons will be strong and brave. Our God is with us. We are warriors."

BE YOUR KIDS' DAD

I was born in Philadelphia in 1940. My mom and dad named me Patrick Livingston Murphy Williams, which were all the Scotch-Irish names that would fit onto one birth certificate. When I was a year and a half old, the Japanese bombed Pearl Harbor. Dad wanted to do his part for the war effort, but his age and poor eyesight kept him out of combat.

When I turned three, he gave me a baseball glove for my birthday. Soon after that, he joined the American Red Cross and shipped out to the Pacific. He returned home in late 1945. I remember waiting at the train station with my mom and sisters. I recall Mom's tearful excitement when a strange man stepped off the train. That stranger was my dad.

Jim Williams was a calm, easy-going man who worked hard and loved his family. He was a caring but firm disciplinarian. I respected his authority and rarely crossed it. For those few times that I foolishly provoked his ire, Dad kept a big paint paddle on the kitchen wall—his "Patrick Persuader."

I was seven years old when my youngest sister, Mary Ellen, was born. By then, I already had two sisters and no brothers, and I really wanted a little brother to play ball with! I didn't understand that there were deeper problems surrounding Mary Ellen's birth. Only later did I understand that she was born with severe mental retardation—what are now called cognitive disabilities.

Mom and Dad faced this challenge together and became involved in fundraising activities to help educate Delawarians about Down syndrome children. My dad and his friend Bob Carpenter, owner of the Philadelphia Phillies, cofounded an annual football tournament to benefit research and care for the mentally retarded.

While I was growing up in Wilmington, Delaware, Dad taught and coached at Tower Hill School, a private all-grade school. Dad's job didn't pay well, but at least he could send me to Tower Hill free of charge. When I was in the sixth grade, Dad resigned at Tower Hill and began selling life insurance. I was devastated. Why would anyone quit *coaching* just to sell something as boring as *insurance*! But Dad made good money in insurance because of his likable, outgoing personality.

Dad often talked about the value of hard work. For six years, he got up early and drove me around on my paper route. He also went to my games, where he took countless snapshots and home movies. He'd whoop and holler and tell everybody, "That's my boy!" It was embarrassing! I thought, *Oh, Dad, knock it off! What are the guys going to think?* But looking back, I realize how lucky I was to have such an involved father.

Dad, You're Important!

While researching a previous book, *Coaching Your Kids to Be Leaders*, I conducted over 800 interviews with men and women from all walks of life.[1] One question I asked was, "Who most influenced your life?" The response I repeatedly heard was "my dad." This doesn't take anything away from the influence of moms. Mothers play an enormous role in shaping a child's character, sense of security and emotional well-being. But I believe fathers have the greatest role to play in helping a child face the challenges, obstacles, dangers and rough-and-tumble realities of the world.

My dad, Jim Williams, was my first and most important role model. He took me to my first big-league game when I was seven years old. I still have vivid memories of that game—the Cleveland Indians versus the Philadelphia Athletics in a double-header at Shibe Park. I yelled my head off, gobbled down hot dogs, and became hooked on sports for life.

If you're a father, you're important. You're an irreplaceable and indispensable part of your child's life.

That one afternoon set the course of my adult life. I have lived my life in the sports world because my Dad imbued me with a love of athletic competition.

Dad was my first coach. My earliest and fondest memories are of times I spent with him in the Tower Hill locker room or on the bench by the field. I heard him give a lot of motivational speeches, and I absorbed his enthusiasm, his ideals and his values. If my dad had not come back from the war, or if he had not been a loving, affirming, involved father, my life would be very different today.

Kids need their dads. If you're a father, you're important. You're an irreplaceable and indispensable part of your child's life. Let me tell you about a very famous guy who had to grow up without his dad.

In May 2005, Yankee third baseman Alex Rodriguez revealed to the world that he has some serious problems—problems that even his $252 million, 10-year contract can't fix. Because of those problems, the highest-paid player in baseball had been seeing two different therapists.

Rodriguez, better known as "A-Rod," was born of Dominican parents in New York City, not far from Yankee Stadium. His parents moved to the Dominican Republic for a while, then to Miami. From his dad, a semi-pro baseball player, young Alex learned to love the game. But his dad also inflicted on him one of the worst wounds a child can suffer. When Alex was nine, his father abandoned the family.

Alex's mother raised him and his two siblings by working two jobs; she was a secretary by day and a waitress by night. Alex helped his mom count up her tips every night. The pain of his father's rejection haunted Alex throughout his childhood and on into adulthood. "I thought he was coming back," he told an interviewer. "But he never came back. It still hurts."

Some might say that A-Rod's phenomenal success as a baseball player can be attributed, in part, to the pain he suffered at age nine. It could be that his father's neglect drove A-Rod to seek praise, affirmation and attention from the crowds. Maybe the emptiness inside him spurred him on to greatness as a baseball player. But what a price to pay for fame!

The world is full of abandoned, neglected, fatherless kids, and few of them ever achieved greatness. In fact, all too many of them now populate our prisons, crack houses, homeless shelters and gutters. The abandonment they experienced didn't drive them to the top; it dragged them to the bottom.

How did A-Rod achieve greatness in spite of his pain? I would give credit to the two men in his life who stepped into the place his father vacated. One was Alex's stepfather, who encouraged him to work through his anger with physical training. This man took young Alex to school two hours early every day. From 5 to 7 A.M., Alex worked out in the gym, doing push-ups, sit-ups, weight training and playing ball.

The other substitute dad in A-Rod's life was Eddie "El Gallo" Rodriguez, Alex's mentor at the Boys and Girls Club in Miami (despite the last name, El Gallo and A-Rod are not related). Because of El Gallo's impact on his life, A-Rod has given over a million dollars to Boys and Girls Clubs all across America.

Though A-Rod's father wounded him, his substitute dads showed him how to channel his pain into achievement. The pain is still there— that's why he's in therapy. But the pain didn't destroy him, because there were two men in his life who cared.

Every child needs a dad (or a substitute dad). The genetic link doesn't matter. All that matters is the emotional bond, the affirmation and the love. Every child needs a father who will say, "You have value. You can do anything you set your mind to—and I'll be here to help you along the way."

YOUR NUMBER ONE JOB

NBA legend Karl Malone (Utah Jazz, L.A. Lakers) was probably the best power forward to ever play pro basketball. He is also an all-pro dad. "We sit out here around the pool," he once said during his playing days. "My kids are playing and that's when I'm the happiest. I ask them, 'You kids want to watch Daddy play basketball today or you want to watch the *Aladdin* show on TV?' They say, '*Aladdin*! Go have a good game, Daddy!'

"That keeps everything in perspective for me, because to my kids, I'm just Dad. I doubt if my kids will remember Daddy playing basketball. What they'll remember is that I went walking with them, I went swimming with them, I tucked them in at night. That's what it's all about for me."

That's what it's all about for every dad. Many busy, successful fathers think they are defined by the work they do, by their bank accounts, their titles, their job descriptions, their awards. But as news commentator Cal Thomas once observed, "I have known five presidents, traveled throughout much of the world, had the heady experience of being asked for my autograph, and enjoyed the praise of a small number of people. None of that has meant as much as the hugs and kisses I have received from my children (and wife!) and the voluntary acknowledgments of their love for me. You can't hang that on the wall to impress colleagues, but you can hide it in your heart to comfort you in your old age."

Dr. David Jeremiah, senior pastor of Shadow Mountain Community Church near San Diego, California, is a father and grandfather. "There are others who can counsel," he once said, "others who can make personnel decisions, others who can orchestrate the organization, but there is only one man in the whole world who can be a father to my children—and that's me. I had better be that father while I have the opportunity."

Millionaire entrepreneur Jeno Paulucci created more than seventy businesses or brands during his seven-decade career: Chun King, Jeno's, Luigino's, Michelina's, Budget Gourmet, and many more. He has served as an advisor to every American president from Eisenhower to George W. Bush. "If I had to do my life over again," Paulucci once said, "I'd do it differently. Why? Because I never knew my family. I've got three wonderful children, four wonderful grandchildren, and a wonderful wife of forty-one years. When you work seven days a week, fighting to survive, fighting to grow, you sacrifice something. I believe the sacrifice was too great for being listed in *Forbes*. I'd rather take *Forbes* and tear it up, and have grown up with my children, because life is so short."

These four leaders from the world of sports, media, religion and business are saying the same thing in different ways: What good does it do to have fame, a corner office, and a six-figure income if you're a stranger to your family? No amount of success can make up for failure in the home.

Not long ago, I was sitting amid all the beaux-arts splendor of the grand ballroom of the Willard InterContinental Hotel, just two blocks from the White House. The featured speaker was First Lady Laura Bush.

What am I doing here? I wondered. *I'm a pair of old running shoes in a roomful of tuxedoes!*

It was April 19, 2005, and the National Fatherhood Initiative (NFI) had invited me to its annual Fatherhood Awards Gala in Washington, D.C. Along with country music star Buddy Jewell, Fox News analyst Fred Barnes and Atlanta Falcons defensive back Allen Rossum, I was there to receive an award given to men who exemplify involved and committed fatherhood. *Well*, I thought, *I'm probably getting an award for quantity, not quality.*

Granted, there aren't too many guys in the world who are "Dad" to 19 kids. But looking back over my years as a father, I'm keenly aware of the times I've failed, the times I should have been more strict or less strict, the times I should have listened more and talked less, the times I should have given better advice or guided with a firmer hand. I thought, *Boy, if the good people of NFI could see some of the king-size goofs I've made as a dad, they wouldn't give me an award—they'd escort me out of the building!*

It was quite an evening. First, R&B performer Cincere performed a song called "Daddy," with a children's chorus that sang the refrain, "Daddy, Daddy, Daddy, come home!" Okay, I admit it, that song put a lump in my throat and a tear in my eye.

Then the First Lady got up to speak. "Across America," she said, "twenty-four million children live apart from their father. Forty percent of these children haven't seen their father in the last year. As Roland Warren has said, 'Kids have a hole in their soul the shape of their dad.'

"Statistics show that when children grow up without a mom and dad at home, they're more likely to fall behind in school, more likely to experiment with drugs and alcohol, more likely to be in trouble with the law. And boys who grow up without fathers are more likely to become fathers themselves at a young age, perpetuating a cycle of absentee fatherhood that has terrible consequences, generation after generation. The evidence is clear: Children need fathers in their lives."

Mrs. Bush talked about visiting a place called Rosalie Manor in Milwaukee, which runs a program called Today's Dads. The program mentors teen fathers to become responsible dads. She told about Ken, one of the young men she met in the Today's Dads program.

Ken grew up with drug-addicted parents, surrounded by a culture of crime and drug abuse. When his girlfriend became pregnant, Ken decided he wanted to give his son a better life than he'd had. With the help of the Today's Dads program, Ken stopped selling drugs and got a job delivering pizzas. Working nights, he could stay home with the baby during the day. Fatherhood is a daily struggle for Ken. Selling drugs was easy money; delivering pizzas is hard work. But Ken wants to be a man—and a father.

"Every father faces challenges, regardless of his circumstances," the First Lady concluded. "The father who's absent because he's in prison or the father who's absent because he works 80 hours a week both have children who wish they could see their dads more."

It's true. If you're a father, then you had better be a *hands-on* father. No other goal or obligation in your life even comes close. Fatherhood is your number one job. That's not just the message of Pat Williams. That's the message of Asher's life and legacy. And it's a message straight from the heart of the ultimate Father, God Himself.

EVERY KID NEEDS A DAD

While this book was being written, I had a fascinating experience. I had two speaking engagements on the same day, both before groups of young people. At 8:45 in the morning, I spoke to around 300 students who had come to Orlando from all over the southeastern United States. They were among the brightest, sharpest kids in the country, and they had come for an intensive four-day leadership program at Student Leadership University. SLU, founded by my friend Jay Strack, is one of the best leadership training programs in the country. The event was held at a beautiful resort hotel on International Drive.

After my talk, I met many of the young people and was very impressed. A short time later, I drove to my next stop, just a few miles away. Again, my

If you're a father, then you had better be a *hands-on* father. No other goal or obligation in you life even comes close.

audience consisted of teenagers—but with one big difference: These teens were at the Orange County Jail.

Housing almost 3,500 prisoners, the Orange County Jail is the fifteenth largest facility of its kind in the country. I was there to talk to 30 young men who had been jailed for an assortment of crimes: drug dealing, burglary, armed robbery, and, in some cases, murder.

The prison chaplain, Bernard Fleeks, filled me in on the lives of these young offenders. There were two common threads that ran through almost every case: First, there was no father in their homes. Second, these offenders had succumbed to peer pressure. As I stood in front of that group, I thought, *I can't believe it! They all look like little boys!*

One of them was an 18-year-old who was sentenced to life for taking part in a murder. He told Chaplain Fleeks, "I didn't do it!" And he was probably telling the truth. But he was at the crime scene and he got caught, so he's going to pay for that mistake for the rest of his life.

Chaplain Fleeks told me that he'd had them all write an essay on how they felt about their lives. Almost all of those essays expressed bitterness about a father who wasn't there or wasn't interested or was abusive. The award-winning essay was given to the news media. Someone in the media tracked down the father of the young offender who had written it. This father was remorseful and admitted he'd neglected his son. In fact, he wrote back to his son and said, in effect, "I know I hurt you by neglecting you. The whole time you were growing up, I was out on the streets doing the same things that put you in jail. I'm sorry. I wish I'd done things differently."

My friend Bill Glass, the former pro football great, has spent the last 35 years conducting prison ministry across America. He's held evangelistic crusades in well over a thousand prisons. I once asked Bill, "Is there a common denominator among all the prisoners you've met?"

"Absolutely," he said. "They all have a father problem. Either they never knew their dad or they were abused or neglected by their dad. To put it bluntly, they all hate their fathers. The greeting card companies donate cards to the prisons for Mother's Day and Father's Day. On Mother's Day, all the cards are snatched up. But on Father's Day, the same number of cards are put out, and they go untouched. What does that tell you about the way these guys feel about their fathers?"

There was a time, and it wasn't long ago, when the prevailing assumption was that children needed mothers but that fathers were optional. The idea that kids do better in school, relationships and life when raised by *both* a mom and a dad was considered controversial and even politically incorrect. However, social and psychological research is mounting that proves that both boys and girls need their dads.

The National Fatherhood Initiative has spent a decade analyzing social trends regarding fatherhood. Here are some of the findings:

- Twenty-four million American children (over a third of all kids in the United States) live in homes without their biological fathers.
- The absence of a dad from so many homes plays a direct role in a number of social ills. Kids in father-deprived homes are more likely to be abused, poor, prone to drug abuse, prone to poor scholastic achievement, and prone to emotional and behavior problems including suicide and crime.
- A study of violent criminals in U.S. prisons showed that prison populations are overwhelmingly made up of males who grew up without fathers. Sixty percent of convicted rapists, 72 percent of adolescent murderers, and 70 percent of all long-term prison inmates came from fatherless homes.
- About 40 percent of kids in homes without dads have not seen their father even once in the past 12 months. More than one-fourth of all absent fathers live out of state from their children. Half of all kids living in father-absent homes never even visit their father's home.
- The rate of child abuse in single-parent families is almost double that in intact two-parent homes. Teens from father-absent homes are twice as likely to use illegal drugs as teens from intact, married-couple families. Kids from single-parent homes are five times as likely to live in poverty as kids from intact, married-couple families.[2]

C. S. Lewis once observed that "fatherhood must be at the core of the universe" because the Creator of the universe is Himself a Father. In fact, Lewis said, the Christian faith teaches us that "the relation of [God the] Father and [God the] Son is of all relations the most central." So when we see the role of fathers disparaged and downgraded in our culture today, it is nothing less than an attack on the natural order of the universe.

THE TRAGEDY OF FAILED FATHERS

In his biography *A Golfer's Life*, Arnold Palmer talks about growing up in Youngstown, Pennsylvania, the son of Deacon Palmer, the head golf pro at the Latrobe Country Club. Arnold's dad, whom he called Pap, was a strict but loving father. Deacon Palmer set the course for Arnold's legendary career when Arnold was just four. He cut down a set of golf clubs to tyke-size and taught Arnie how to swing them. Throughout Arnold Palmer's early years, he revered his father and worked hard to earn Pap's praise.

Deacon Palmer was not a bad man, but he did have a self-destructive weakness: booze. Once, when Arnold had just turned 16, his dad came home after knocking back a few drinks with his buddies. As sometimes happened when he'd been drinking, Deacon Palmer began verbally abusing Arnold's mother.

"It troubled me," Arnold Palmer recalled, "that the man who rode me so hard about knowing the difference between right and wrong often did something—after too many shots at the firehall—he knew was wrong."

Sixteen-year-old Arnie decided enough was enough. He stepped between his mom and dad. "I remember how he looked at me," he recalled, "with surprise and then rage. It was unthinkable that I would challenge him in his house. Almost before I knew what hit me, Pap grabbed me by the shirt and lifted me off the floor with those massive hands of his, and slammed me against a galvanized stovepipe, flattening it against the wall."

That night, Arnie left the house for a while, returning home before dawn. "In the morning," he recalled, "my father didn't say a word about the incident . . . and he never laid a hand on me in anger again, either."[3]

The apostle Paul tells us, "Fathers, do not exasperate your children; instead, bring them up in the training and instruction of the Lord" (Eph. 6:4). The message of this verse is so important that I think it's worth looking at in a couple of additional translations. In the *New Living Translation*, this verse tells us, "And now a word to you fathers. Don't make your children angry by the way you treat them. Rather, bring them up with the discipline and instruction approved by the Lord." And in *THE MESSAGE*, we read, "Fathers, don't exasperate your children by coming down hard on them. Take them by the hand and lead them in the way of the Master."

As fathers, we are called by God to be firm but fair, not exasperating our kids by getting on their backs, but leading them and guiding them in the way of Jesus, our Lord and Master.

The pages of Scripture are strewn with tragic examples of men who failed as fathers. Take, for example, the Old Testament priest Eli. He was one of the last leaders of Israel in the time of the Judges, before Israel's first kings. Eli loved God and delighted in serving the Lord. He trained a young man named Samuel and mentored him to become a great prophet in Israel.

But though Eli had a godly influence on young Samuel, he failed to bring up his own two sons to follow in his righteous footsteps. Eli's sons, Hophni and Phinehas, were wicked priests who had no reverence for God. "Eli's sons were wicked men," the Bible tells us. "They had no regard for the Lord" (1 Sam. 2:12). These men disgraced their calling in various ways, including engaging in immoral conduct on the premises of God's holy tabernacle. God eventually struck them down in judgment.

Though Eli tried to confront his sons, his anemic rebuke had no effect on his sons' behavior. Eli asked, "Why do you do such things?" (v. 23) but he didn't tell them to stop. He didn't warn them of God's judgment. And his sons didn't take him seriously. They treated their father's feeble rebuke as a joke and went on their merry way. Later, the Lord said this about Eli and his sons: "[Eli's] sons made themselves contemptible, and he failed to restrain them" (1 Sam. 3:13). Eli could have intervened, but he didn't. He failed as a father.

And what about Eli's protégé, Samuel? He became a great leader in Israel, the last of the Old Testament judges, the man God chose to anoint the first kings of Israel. Samuel led the nation through the wars against the Philistines. He built an altar and established regular worship at Shiloh. Samuel was a statesman, a reformer, and a prophet—but he failed as a father.

Samuel installed his sons as judges in Beersheba, but they were evil and took bribes in exchange for dishonest judgments. Because Samuel's sons were so corrupt, the people lost faith in the rule of the judges. They gathered around Samuel and said, "You are old, and your sons do not walk in your ways; now appoint a king to lead us, such as all the other nations have" (1 Sam. 8:5).

So the people of Israel got the king they demanded—yet this king, named Saul, turned out to be a bitter disappointment to both God and Israel. All of this took place because Samuel failed as a father.

Eventually King Saul was succeeded by King David. David was a great king, a mighty warrior, a renowned poet, and beloved by his people. As a father, however, King David was a spectacular failure.

David's eldest son, Amnon, raped David's daughter Tamar. In response, another son, Absalom, murdered Amnon. Fearing David's wrath, Absalom fled into exile. Eventually, Absalom conspired against his father and raised up an army of rebels, forcing his father to flee. After David spent some time in exile, Absalom was killed and David returned to the throne—but it was a hollow victory for David.

"O my son Absalom!" David wept when he heard that his son was dead. "My son, my son Absalom! If only I had died instead of you—O Absalom, my son, my son!" (2 Sam. 18:33). That's the cry of a man who knows he has failed as a father.

Please understand: You may have a child who has wandered from the faith, or who has turned his back on you, or who has gotten involved in immoral or criminal behavior—but that does *not* mean, in and of itself, that you have failed as a father. Every child has free will and can choose to reject everything you diligently try to teach him or her. Kids have many influences tugging at them, including godless peers, an immoral and irreligious media barrage, and their own selfish desires. Sometimes, the kids of good, involved, loving fathers simply choose to go the wrong way.

Also, I want you to know that every dad makes mistakes. I've sure made my share, and I'm grateful that God's grace has covered most of them. Every dad—myself included—reaches a point where, with the benefit of 20/20 hindsight, he wishes he had made some different choices as a father. But the fact that our kids didn't walk in the path we pointed out to them is not necessarily evidence of failure; rather, it's proof that we are fallen people living in a fallen world.

The only man who is truly a failure as a father is the man who fails to love and guide his kids, to be there for them, to pray for them, to lovingly discipline them, to affirm them and teach them God's plan for their lives. My point here is not to accuse you or anyone else of having failed; it's to encourage you to succeed and to become the father God meant for you to be.

HOW TO BE A PERFECT DAD

We all want to be the perfect dad—a Ward Cleaver-ish sort of fellow with a touch of gray at the temples, a man who can always be found in his wood-paneled den, puffing on his pipe, ready to dispense fatherly wisdom to his kids on any subject from how to build a kite to understanding girls to the simplest proof of the Pythagorean theorem. There isn't anything he doesn't know and there isn't any problem he can't fix.

Don't you want to be a perfect dad? Sure you do! To help you reach that goal, I've assembled a simple guide to flawless fatherhood. Follow these easy steps and you, too, can achieve perfection as a father.

Step 1: Forget About Being Perfect
Instead of trying to be the perfect dad, be honest and real. Dads are human and make mistakes. When you make a mistake, own up to it honestly. If it's

The only man who is a failure as a father is the man who fails to love and guide his kids, be there for them, pray for them, lovingly discipline them, affirm them and teach them God's plan for their lives.

minor and harmless, laugh at yourself and move on. If you did something hurtful to your kids, such as yelling at them when you shouldn't have or missing one of their important events, then admit it and apologize sincerely.

Some dads seem to feel that saying "I was wrong, I'm sorry, please forgive me" will diminish them in their children's eyes. Wrong! Admitting your flaws and asking forgiveness *increases* the respect and love they'll have for you. Acknowledging mistakes actually *magnifies* you in their eyes. I guarantee it: Every child's image of the "perfect dad" is a dad who's big enough to admit he's not perfect.

You want your kids to admit it when they do wrong, don't you? Then set an example. When you mess up, *fess up*! If your kids catch you in an inconsistency, don't try to explain how what you did doesn't count. Admit that you were inconsistent and ask forgiveness.

Arthur Ashe, the late world-class tennis champ, understood this principle well. In an interview he gave shortly before he died in 1993 of complications from AIDS (contracted from a tainted blood transfusion during heart surgery), Ashe talked about parenting by example.

"My wife and I talk about this with our six-year-old daughter," he said. "Children are much more impressed by what they see you do than by what you say. They keep you honest. If you've been preaching one thing all along, and you don't do it, all of a sudden they'll bring it right up in your face.

"I tell my daughter it's not polite to eat with your elbows on the table. Then, after dinner, I'm putting my elbows up. She says, 'Daddy, your elbows are on the table.' You have to be man enough to say 'you're right' and take your elbows down. In fact that's an even stronger learning experience than just telling her in words. When she calls me on it, I know she's listening . . . and when I admit I was wrong, she knows her daddy is man enough to be consistent."

Step 2: Be the Dad Your Kids Need

Dad is no less important than Mom. Your kids need you—and your daughter needs you as much as your son. Even if you are divorced from your kids' mother, find a way to be involved and available for your kids.

Don't deprive them of the time, affirmation, guidance and love that only you can give them.

Step 3: Affirm Your Kids

Use affirming words: "I love you! I'm proud of you! You're awesome!" Give them an affirming touch: Hug them, put your arm around your kids' shoulders, and get down on the floor and wrestle with them. Your touch says, "I like you. I enjoy being around you. I want to connect with you."

Be an affirming presence in the lives of your kids. Go to their games, recitals, school plays, and every other event that is important to them. Show you value them by sacrificing some of your interests in order to be with them at the key moments of their lives.

That's the kind of father Cal Ripken, Sr., was—a blue-collar guy, a longtime coach and manager in the Baltimore Orioles baseball organization. When his son, Cal Ripken, Jr., was just a little tyke, Cal, Sr., would get the boy out of bed before sunrise and they'd have a quick breakfast together. Then they'd drive to the ballpark where Cal, Jr., would watch and listen as his dad coached.

Years later, Cal, Jr., became one of the legendary players of the game, playing shortstop for the Orioles. On September 6, 1995, Cal Ripken, Jr., broke Lou Gehrig's record of 2,130 consecutive games played (a streak he later extended to 2,632). The night Cal, Jr., broke the record, he stepped onto the field at Camden Yards and looked up to the skybox. There was Cal, Sr., beaming with pride at his son's achievement. Cal, Jr., later said, "It seemed like there was an exchange of a million words without saying one." Cal, Jr., knows what it's like to have an affirming father; his dad showed what it's like to be one.

Step 4: Listen to Your Kids

Set aside regular time each day to talk to each of your children—and to *listen*. Don't just wait for opportunities; *make* opportunities happen. As your children talk, make eye contact. Give them nonverbal feedback—a nod or grin to show you're giving your full attention. Even a preschooler knows when you are just saying, "Uh-huh, that's nice," while watching TV or reading your e-mail. Kids know when they're being patronized, and it makes them feel demeaned and unimportant.

When listening to your children, don't just listen to the words. Listen for emotions, fears and unspoken messages. For example, after the 9/11 terrorist attacks in 2001, a first-grade boy asked, "Daddy, were there children in those buildings?" The father replied, "I'm sure there were only grownups in those buildings, and most of them got out okay." Over the next few days, the boy asked the same question several more times. Finally, the dad realized what the boy was really asking: "Am I safe, or could an airplane fly into my house?" He just didn't know how to put the question into words. Once the dad grasped the child's unspoken question, he could help the boy feel secure.

Never make your child feel stupid for asking a question or expressing an opinion. Kids are easily shamed and intimidated. You want your children to talk so that you can know what they're thinking. So invite them to express their ideas. Ask questions. Be a good listener.

Step 5: Take Time to Be a Dad

Find creative ways to spend time with your kids. Turn a business trip into a family trip. Turn a solitary chore, like weekend gardening or cleaning out the garage, into a fun project with your kids. Take your kids with you on errands and trips to the hardware store.

After Mother Teresa was awarded the Nobel Peace Prize, a reporter asked her, "What can we do to help promote world peace?" She replied, "Go home and love your family." The best way to love your kids is to spend *time* with them—lots and lots of time.

It's often said that children are the future, and we have to think about what they will become. But I think we sometimes forget that our children are also the present. We need to think about who they are *today* and what they are thinking and going through *right now*. The only way we can do that is by giving them the gift of our time. Spending time with your kids is not an obligation. It's a privilege.

Step 6: Support Your Wife's Role as Mom

Never do anything that would diminish her in the kids' eyes or undermine her parental authority. This is true even if you are divorced.

In disciplinary matters, always coordinate with your kids' mom. If she has parenting skills that you lack, ask her to show you how she does it.

Step 7: Be a Fun Dad

Kids need fun and laughter almost as much as they need love. Make sure they see you as a guy who's fun to be around. Take your kids on roller coasters and water slides. Tell stupid jokes. Have water balloon fights with your kids. Play board games together. Help them build kites, and then go out and fly them. Be a fun dad.

One day when my daughter Katarina was about 13 or 14, we were sitting around the dining room table. She said, "Dad, why can't you be a casual dad?"

I said, "Kati, what's a casual dad?"

"Well, a casual dad is someone who's fun to be with. He kind of lets up on his kids once in a while. I know you have to have discipline and rules, especially with so many kids in the house. But maybe sometimes you could be a casual dad."

To this day, we still use that phrase in our house. If the kids think I'm coming on with too much structure, they say, "Hey, where's our casual dad? We haven't seen him in a while!" It's convicting—and it's given me a whole new approach to fatherhood. To this day, I find myself thinking, *How am I coming across to my kids? Am I being a casual dad? Am I being fun?*

When Billy Graham was 75, a reporter asked him, "Dr. Graham, what do you want to be remembered for?" And Dr. Graham answered, "I want to be remembered as a dad who was fun to live with."

In his novel *The Edge of Sadness*, Edwin O'Connor writes about an Irish Catholic family in the 1950s. One of the young men in the novel says, "My father didn't drink, much less get drunk. I don't think he ever looked at a woman besides my mother. All of us ate three good meals a day and had no holes in our shoes. He had all the domestic virtues, you see, except that it was hell on earth to live with him." Make sure that you're not "hell on earth" to live with. Among all of your virtues as a father, put *fun* near the top of the list.[4]

Step 8: Follow the Example of the Ultimate Father

We don't have to wonder what the "perfect father" is like. We have the ultimate example of fatherhood right in front of us: God Himself. Though we
find many images of God in the Bible—Creator, Lord, King, Shepherd, and
so forth—the image Jesus impressed upon is that of God the loving Father.

Jesus taught us to pray, "Our Father in heaven" (Matt. 6:9), and when He
prayed, He not only called God "Father," but He also called Him "Abba!" In
Mark 14:36, when Jesus prayed in the garden before going to the cross, He
prayed, "Abba, Father   everything is possible for you. Take this cup
from me. Yet not what I will, but what you will." That Aramaic word "Abba"
literally means "Daddy!" and is the word a little child would call out when
running up and jumping into his daddy's lap. Jesus wants us to know that
God is our heavenly Daddy and we can crawl up in His lap anytime we want.
And that's the kind of daddy you and I should be to our kids.

The most powerful portrayal of the fatherhood of God is the parable
Jesus told about the prodigal son and the loving father. The word "prodigal" means "carelessly, wastefully extravagant," and this famous story of
the wasteful son and his forgiving father is probably the best loved of all the
parables of Jesus.

This story, found in Luke 15:11-32, tells of a thoughtless son who goes
to his dad and says, "Father, give me my share of the estate" (v. 12). In other
words, "Dad, I'm tired of waiting around for you to die so I can get what's
coming to me. Divide up everything you own, and give me my share." What
an insult! This brash young man practically tells his dad, "I wish you were
dead!" Nothing could be more offensive.

But the father ignores the insult and gives the son what he demands.
The boy takes his money and leaves without a backward glance. He goes to
a far country and wastes the money on sinful living. Soon, a famine strikes
the land and, in desperation, this Jewish boy ends up doing something no
self-respecting Jew would ever do: He takes a job slopping the hogs. In those
days, any Jew who took care of pigs was considered cursed, because pigs
were "unclean" under Jewish law.

Finally, the boy decides to beg his father to take him back—not as a son,
but as a hired servant. So he returns home. At this point, Jesus inserts a fascinating detail. He says, "But while [the boy] was still a long way off, his

father saw him and was filled with compassion for him" (v. 20). How did this father happen to see his boy while he was "a long way off"? Clearly, the father had a habit of rising every morning, going out on a hill, and looking for his son. He eagerly hoped his boy would return.

What does the father do when he sees his son? He runs to the boy, throws his arms around him, and kisses him! Then he calls his servants and has them bring out the best robe for the boy, puts a gold ring on the boy's finger, and throws a huge party.

And here's the lesson of this story for you and me: No matter what that boy did, no matter how he had sinned and degraded himself, no matter how ungrateful and wasteful he had been, the boy was unconditionally loved by his father. When he was still a long way off, his father ran to meet him and welcome him home. This father was so joyful that he cried out, "This son of mine was dead and is alive again; he was lost and is found" (v. 32).

That's just a glimpse into the heart of our loving heavenly Father. That's just a taste of the great love He has shown you and me. The more we get to know the God of the Bible, the more we learn to see Him as the loving Father He is—and the more we want to pattern ourselves after His example. In God the Father, we see the ultimate model of fatherly authority, affection, forgiveness and generosity.

God is exactly the kind of father you and I want to become—the kind of father we *must* become. God is the ultimate example of a father who influences generations of heads of families, choice men, brave warriors, and outstanding leaders. Asher was a great father because he followed in the footsteps of God the Father.

THE DEFINITION OF A FATHER

On Father's Day 1998, Ben Stein was interviewed on CNN about his book on fatherhood, *Tommy and Me: The Making of a Dad*.[5] You know Ben

God is exactly the kind of father you and I want to become—
the kind of father we *must* become.

Stein. As an actor, he played the droning teacher in *Ferris Bueller's Day Off*. He has also been a columnist, novelist, quiz show host (Comedy Central's *Win Ben Stein's Money*), and a White House speechwriter.

Interviewed by CNN's Bobbie Battista, he talked about the process of adopting his son Tommy. "It was quite a struggle to get him," Stein said. "And once we had him, it wasn't easy for me to be a dad. I felt kind of estranged and inadequate."

One obstacle Stein had to overcome was his fear that he wasn't up to the job. "I felt I probably wouldn't be a good dad," he said. "I wasn't a good athlete. I wasn't particularly inspiring or strong personality-wise."

Stein points to one incident as the moment he truly saw himself as a father. "One night, after maybe about a year and a half or two years of being a very bad and absent father," he said, "I was telling Tommy a story. I guess he must have been two and a half or three. I told him this little story and I said, 'Well, good night, Tommy,' thinking he might go, 'Goo-goo.' And he said, with perfect pitch and punctuation, 'Good night, Daddy,' in the sweetest voice I've ever heard. And I was simply putty in his hands from then on. There's nothing that I wouldn't do for him after that."

Stein also credits Dr. James Dobson of Focus on the Family for helping him understand the fatherhood role. He paraphrased Dobson's counsel this way: "Don't worry if you're not the best athlete on the block. Your kid wants to be with you. If you will just pay attention to him, he will be a boundless reservoir of love and affection for you."

Referring to his role as a finance and economics analyst on the cable news networks, Stein added, "I'm often on business shows and people say to me, 'What's a good investment now?' And I always say, 'The best investment is to go home from work early and spend the afternoon throwing a ball around with your son. That's a really good investment. The returns on it are tax-free. There's no possibility that you'll lose on it. And your son will reap enormous benefits from it.'"

I'm so glad Ben Stein is writing and talking about being an adoptive father. I want everyone to know about the millions of kids in this world who need a loving, secure home. I want everyone to know that this relationship called *adoption* has a special place of honor in God's Word and in His heart. Our God is an adoptive Father.

In our culture, people tend to dismiss adoption as a second-class relationship. Sometimes people will ask me, "Is so-and-so one of your *real* kids or one of your *adopted* kids?" Hey, they're *all* my real kids! In his book *Twice Adopted*, radio personality Michael Reagan puts it his way:

Unfortunately, we live in a society which has long viewed adoption as an "abnormal" or "second-best" family arrangement. Even in the church, we have accepted this notion that adoption is a deviation from the norm. Even in Christian families, siblings sometimes tease each other, joking, "Oh, didn't Mom and Dad ever tell you that you were adopted?" Behind this teasing is the assumption that an adopted kid is different and inferior—a misfit.[6]

That's not how God views adoption. In both the Old and New Testaments, God takes an elevated view of adoption. Look at the story of Moses in Exodus 2:1-10. There, Moses, a Hebrew baby, is given up to be adopted by Pharaoh's daughter in order to save his life. Only by being adopted as an Egyptian could Moses become the liberator of the Hebrews.

And the New Testament tells us that we can't become God's children unless we are adopted into God's family! Nobody was ever *born* a Christian; we only become Christians by *adoption*. As the apostle Paul explained, "So you should not be like cowering, fearful slaves. You should behave instead like God's very own children, adopted into his family—calling him 'Father, dear Father'" (Rom. 8:15, *NLT*).

God has brought us into His home and showered us with His love. Again, Michael Reagan observes:

Christians don't take a back seat to God's "birth kids," because He doesn't have birth kids. His entire family is an adoptive family. You can't get into God's family any other way. We start life as slaves, and we are adopted as God's sons and heirs. God gives us the right to crawl up into his lap and whisper in His ear, because He has redeemed us and adopted us as His children.[7]

I believe we should all reprogram our thinking about what "fatherhood" really means. Instead of defining a father as "a man who procreates," we would instead say, "a father is a man who loves, nurtures, trains, mentors, teaches, disciplines, affirms, cares for, and provides for a child, regardless of whether or not he is genetically connected to that child." There are many ways to be a father and a spiritual descendent of Asher. You don't have to be the genetic male parent of a child to fulfill that role. You can voluntarily become the father figure in the lives of young people who do not have a father.

FATHERHOOD IS A HOLY CALLING

In November 2001, I was in Boston promoting *How to Be Like Mike*, my book on the life of NBA legend Michael Jordan.[8] In the morning, I appeared on a local TV show. That evening, I went to the Fleet Center to watch Michael and the Washington Wizards take on the Boston Celtics. I had a chance to visit with Mike in the locker room before the game. He greeted me warmly and said he'd seen me on TV that morning, promoting the book.

"Hey, Williams," he kidded, "you're telling all my stories!"

I laughed and said, "You know, Mike, I have been getting raves from readers all over the country. They say, 'When you see Mike, thank him for being such a role model.'"

Jordan grinned and said, "You know something? I'm just a product of my mom and dad. I represent them. Everything I am today is just a result of the way James and Deloris Jordan raised me and the things they taught me."

What a tribute that is! It sounds exactly like something the sons, grandsons and great-grandsons of Asher might have said.

Before David Robinson retired from the NBA in 2003, he was one of the best centers in pro basketball. Nicknamed "The Admiral" because of his service in the U.S. Navy, Robinson is an outspoken Christian, an outstanding leader, a choice man of God, and a great father. The number one NBA draft pick in 1987, he played his entire career with the San Antonio Spurs. He led his team to NBA championships in 1999 and 2003.

Sports writer Phil Taylor recalled a special moment after Robinson and the Spurs won their first NBA championship in 1999, defeating the New York Knicks in five games. Writing in *Sports Illustrated,* Taylor said that Robinson was getting dressed in the visitors' locker room at Madison Square Garden. The game of Robinson's life had ended only an hour and a half earlier. There were reporters all around, eager to interview The Admiral after his huge career-capping victory.

But the reporters had to wait. Robinson was not taking their questions yet. He was busy answering the questions of his six-year-old son, David, Jr.

"How do you tie a tie, Daddy?" David, Jr., asked.

"Well," the NBA champ replied, "you bring this part around here and tuck this in here and then you pull down here."

"Is it hard?" the boy asked.

"Not once you know how to do it. Don't worry, I'll teach you."

Phil Taylor recalled that the father and son went on chatting as if they were the only two people in that room. "On the night that he reached the peak of his profession," the sports writer concluded, "Robinson was content to be the Dad of David, Jr."[9]

Some years ago, I had dinner with Campus Crusade for Christ founder Bill Bright and his wife, Vonette. It was right after they had moved to Orlando and they wanted to know how we managed our huge household. I explained some of the rules, procedures and discipline we had instilled in order to keep things in line.

After listening carefully, Bill gently said, "Don't forget the love."

I always remembered that. Yes, a household needs order, but kids need love. While setting up your rules and discipline, don't forget the love.

Being a father is the job of a lifetime. That's true whether you are a birth father, an adoptive father, a stepfather, or a substitute father. Becoming a father changes you in ways you could never imagine before. It makes you richer and wiser. It deepens your soul. It teaches you about the true depths of human love.

Fatherhood is a holy calling. Don't turn your back on it. Answer your calling. Be a spiritual descendent of Asher and a warrior for the hearts of your kids. Be their dad.

Notes
1. Pat Williams, *Coaching Your Kids to Be Leaders* (Nashville, TN: Warner Faith, 2005).
2. National Fatherhood Initiative, "NFI Research." http://www.fatherhood.org/research.asp (accessed November 2005).
3. Arnold Palmer with James Dodson, *A Golfer's Life* (New York: Ballantine Books, 2000).
4. Edwin O'Connor, *The Edge of Sadness* (Chicago, IL: Loyola Press, 2005).
5. Ben Stein, *Tommy and Me: The Making of a Dad* (New York: The Free Press, 1998).
6. Michael Reagan with Jim Denny, *Twice Adopted* (Nashville, TN: Broadman and Holman, 2004).
7. Ibid.
8. Pat Williams with Michael Weinreb, *How to be Like Mike: Life Lessons About Basketball's Best* (Deerfield Beach, FL: Health Communications Incorporated, 2001).
9. Phil Taylor, "Here's to You, Mr. Robinson," *Sports Illustrated,* April 7, 2003. http://sports illustrated.cnn.com/si_online/scorecard/news/2003/04/01/sc/ (accessed November 2005).

Raise Godly Kids

In 1962, while in my senior year at Wake Forest University, I was catcher for the baseball team. We had an excellent ball club—good enough to represent the Atlantic Coast Conference in the NCAA regional tournament. The tournament was in Gastonia, North Carolina, in June. I'd have to miss my graduation ceremony at Wake Forest, but if our team got to play in the College World Series in Omaha, it would be worth it.

There were three other schools in Gastonia for the double elimination tournament—Florida, Florida State and West Virginia. We opened against West Virginia and defeated them easily. The next day, we beat Florida. In double elimination play, you have to lose twice to be knocked out of the tournament, and we hadn't lost once. We were sailing to victory—and maybe we were a little overconfident.

My family came down in two cars for our double-header against Florida State—Dad in one car, Mom and my sisters in the other. As the first game got under way, Florida State had already lost a game and was one game away from elimination. That first game was a lot tougher than my teammates and I expected. We lost, 11 to 8.

We played the second game under the lights. After seven innings, we were tied at one run each.

Top of the eighth, I came up to bat. I let a couple of pitches go by, and then I knocked one over the left field fence. Now Wake Forest had a one-run lead. If we could hold that lead for two more innings, we'd advance to the Series.

Bottom of the eighth, there was a close play at the plate. The throw came home, so I ripped off my catcher's mask and planted myself to make the play. The ball bounced in the dirt, hit me in the face, and whizzed behind me. The runner scored.

After nine innings, we were still tied at two and we went into extra innings. We struggled through the tenth, the eleventh, and to the bottom of the twelfth, still tied. Florida State got a runner on second with no outs, and the pressure was on. The next batter let a couple of strikes go by. I put down a signal for a curve ball. Our pitcher, Don Roth, hooked one in. I heard the crack of the bat and my heart broke in pieces. It was a single to left. The runner slid across the plate just before the throw reached my mitt.

It was over. The game, the tournament, the season, my college baseball career, and our hopes for a trip to the College World Series—all over. I was inconsolable. I didn't want to see or talk to anyone.

As I stood there, absorbed in self-pity, I looked up and there was Dad. "Tough break, son," he said.

"Yeah," I said sullenly. "Tough."

"You almost had 'em."

"Yeah. Almost."

Over by the bleachers, Mom and my sisters waved to me. I waved back, but hardly looked in their direction.

"Well," Dad said, "I guess we'll be leaving." He was going to drop my sister Carol off in D.C. and then drive home to Wilmington. Mom and my other sister, Ruthie, were driving straight home.

"Yeah," I said glumly. "See you back home, Dad."

My family drove off and I trudged back to the team bus for the last ride back to Wake Forest.

I wish I had known that I had just seen my dad for the last time. I might have focused less on a baseball game and more on a relationship. I might have felt less sorry for myself and more grateful for my dad. Instead of answering him in terse monosyllables, I might have given him a hug.

I might have even said, "I love you, Dad."

That night, after Dad drove all night and dropped Carol off in D.C., he fell asleep at the wheel somewhere along the Washington/Baltimore Expressway. In the predawn hours of the morning, his car struck a bridge abutment and he was killed instantly.

My father's funeral was a difficult experience for me. It was hard to see him in the casket. Though I had gone to church as a boy, I didn't have a living Christian faith to hold on to. It also hurt to know that I had scarcely said goodbye to him the last time I'd seen him.

I sometimes wonder how I could have lived with my father all those years without appreciating him more and taking the time to know him better. He was a good man, and he was my first and most important role model.

To this day, I see myself as Jim Williams's protégé.

GOOD—OR GODLY?

What do you want for your children?

Many fathers settle for raising their kids to be good or be happy. But as Christian fathers, we should want much more for our kids—and we should expect more from them. We don't just want them to be good or be happy. We want them to be godly. We want them to have a personal relationship with the Creator of the Universe. We want them to make a difference for Christ in a dark and troubled world.

That means it's not enough to raise kids who are merely obedient. We want to disciple our kids to live for God. That's the goal Moses had in mind when he spoke God's words to the nation of Israel:

> Hear, O Israel: The LORD our God, the LORD is one. Love the LORD your God with all your heart and with all your soul and with all your strength. These commandments that I give you today are to be upon your hearts. Impress them on your children. Talk about them when you sit at home and when you walk along the road, when you lie down and when you get up (Deut. 6:4-7).

That is the goal the psalmist Asaph had in mind when he wrote:

> He decreed statutes for Jacob
> and established the law in Israel,
> which he commanded our forefathers
> to teach their children,
> so the next generation would know them,
> even the children yet to be born,

and they in turn would tell their children.
Then they would put their trust in God
and would not forget his deeds
but would keep his commands (Ps. 78:5-7).

There's nothing wrong with wanting our kids to be respectful, courteous, well-behaved, motivated, focused and competent to achieve great things. But these are all secondary goals. Above all of these issues is the one question that our kids should answer early in life: "Do I love the Lord my God with all my heart and with all my soul and with all my strength?"

If our children can honestly and enthusiastically say yes! to that question, then nothing else matters. Their relationship with God trumps every other consideration in life. If they have a living relationship with God, then good behavior, a good attitude, and a life of joy will naturally follow.

In 1 Chronicles 7:40, Asher is described as a man who not only practiced faith and godliness in his own life but who also transmitted a godly faith to his sons, grandsons and generations that followed. "All these were descendents of Asher," we are told, "heads of families, choice men, brave warriors and outstanding leaders. The number of men ready for battle, as listed in their genealogy, was 26,000."

There is a huge contrast between the story of the generations of Asher and the story of the generations in Israel after the death of Joshua. Born a Hebrew slave in Egypt, Joshua became the right-hand man of Moses during Israel's exodus from captivity. A strong military and spiritual leader, Joshua became the successor to Moses and led Israel into the Promised Land. Under Joshua's generalship, the army of Israel conquered the land, drove out the idol-worshiping enemies of God, and apportioned the land among the tribes and families of Israel. The Bible tells us, "The people served the LORD throughout the lifetime of Joshua" (Judg. 2:7).

We are not just trying to make our kids behave, we're also trying to make them Christlike. We're trying to mold and shape their character, attitude, faith and prayer life so that they resemble that of Jesus the Master.

But after the death of Joshua and his generation, life in Israel takes a tragic turn. The Bible records:

> After that whole generation had been gathered to their fathers, another generation grew up, who knew neither the LORD nor what he had done for Israel. Then the Israelites did evil in the eyes of the LORD and served the Baals. They forsook the LORD, the God of their fathers, who had brought them out of Egypt. They followed and worshiped various gods of the peoples around them (vv. 10-12).

Despite his faithfulness, Joshua somehow failed to transmit his faith and godly values to the generations that followed. As a result, the sons, grandsons and great-grandsons of Joshua's generation turned away from God. They "knew neither the LORD nor what he had done for Israel," so they "forsook the LORD, the God of their fathers." What a tragic epitaph!

The rest of Judges 2 goes on to describe the terrible consequences Israel suffered when the sons, grandsons and great-grandsons of Joshua's generation turned away from the Lord. As a direct result of Israel's disobedience, God handed the nation over to its enemies, and Israel suffered defeat after defeat on the battlefield. Foreign raiders came into the land and plundered Israel's farms and towns, carrying people off as slaves.

Even after all of these terrible consequences, the people continued to worship false gods. "Unlike their fathers," the Bible tells us, "they quickly turned from the way in which their fathers had walked, the way of obedience to the LORD's commands" (v. 17).

You might think, *That was then and this is now. God doesn't work that way anymore. He won't hand my nation over to a bunch of Canaanite raiders to plunder us and kill us with swords.* But God doesn't change. If we fail to raise up generations to follow Him, then we can count on this: Our sons, grandsons and great-grandsons will be preyed upon and raided by enemies and destroyers. When people worship idols of power, pleasure, greed, sex, false philosophy and false religion, God hands them over to be raided and plundered.

What kinds of raiders am I talking about? If our children turn away from God, they will be vulnerable to such enemies as pornography, perversion and sex addiction; sexually transmitted diseases; drug addiction and alcoholism; rampant crime; child abuse; poverty and ignorance; and ultimately, the destruction of the soul in eternity.

HOW TO RAISE GODLY KIDS

In *Twice Adopted*, Michael Reagan recalls a memorable experience during a father-son weekend at Hume Lake Christian Camp in the California Sierras. In 1988, Reagan and his 10-year-old son, Cameron, were sitting in the meeting hall as a speaker challenged dads and sons to a deeper relationship with Jesus Christ. At the end of his talk, the speaker invited them all to step forward and sign a pledge of commitment. Michael leaned over to Cameron and said, "Let's go!"

Cameron looked at his dad in horror. "In front of all these guys?" he whispered. "No way!"

"Wouldn't it be great if we could do this together?"

Cameron shook his head no.

But Michael Reagan continued coaxing. Finally, his son said, "All right! I'll do it!" So father and son stood, went up the aisle, and signed the commitment card. (Reagan keeps the card tucked into his Bible to this day.)

That night in their cabin, Michael and his son were in bed. The lights were out and the room was dark and quiet. Michael heard his son say, "Dad? Will Hume Lake Christian Camp still be here 20 years from now?"

"I suppose so. Why?"

"That was really cool tonight, both of us going forward, making that commitment. Maybe someday I can take my son forward like we did tonight."

Michael Reagan concluded by saying he went to sleep with tears in his eyes and a prayer of "Thank You!" in his heart.[1]

Every Christian father should want to raise kids who are not just good but also godly—kids who not only receive the faith of their fathers but who also want to pass that faith down to their own children and to generations to come. How do we raise kids like that? How do we raise a generation of godly kids who want to perpetuate our godly influence in generations to come?

We make *disciples* of our kids.

What does it mean to make disciples? A disciple is a person who receives a teaching or a way of life and then goes out to spread it to others. Disciples pass it on to others, making more disciples. The ultimate model of a disciple-maker is Jesus. By watching how Jesus made disciples of the Twelve, we can see how we should disciple our own children.

As Dr. James Dobson once said, "It's easier to shape a child than to rebuild an adult." We are not just trying to make our kids behave, we're also trying to make them Christlike. We're trying to mold and shape their character, their attitude, their faith and their prayer life so that they resemble that of Jesus the Master.

How did Jesus shape the lives of His disciples? He taught them. He told them stories. He asked them questions that made them think. He set a good example. He gave them tasks and responsibilities. He motivated, empowered and inspired them to become more than they ever dreamed they could be. Here, then, are some specific actions drawn from the life of Jesus that you can take to help shape your children into disciples of Jesus Christ.

Pray for Your Kids and for Yourself

Ask God to open your children's hearts and make them sensitive to what God wants to teach them. Pray that God will impress the character traits of His Son, Jesus, on their lives. Ask God to also make you sensitive to the leading of the Holy Spirit so that He can teach and disciple your kids through the things you do and say. Ask Him to make you sensitive to the needs, feelings and unspoken thoughts of your children. Pray that He would help you to look beyond any annoyances or misbehavior by your kids so that you can see and meet the real spiritual needs of their lives.

Love Your Children Unconditionally

Love your children regardless of their behavior or misbehavior. The Twelve continually failed and disappointed Jesus, yet He continued to love them and disciple them. Your kids will fail and disappoint you, so make sure they know you love them whether they succeed or fail.

And remember, a well-behaved child can be just as spiritually needy as a child who's acting out. Some kids are well-behaved *not* because they have Christ in their lives, but because they have a naturally compliant personality. They're good at looking good, but they may not be any closer to God than the kid who is a constant aggravation. Make sure each of your children has a real relationship with Jesus Christ, and don't be fooled by outward appearances.

Keep the Lines of Communication Open

Throughout the gospels, we see Jesus talking to His disciples. He didn't just preach to them and tell stories to them. He also questioned them and answered their questions. So talk to your kids—and listen to them. Ask open-ended questions that must be answered with complete sentences, not just a one-syllable grunt. The only way to get to know your kids' thoughts, feelings and dreams is by frequent two-way communication.

Seize Every Teachable Moment

The more time you spend with your kids, the more teaching opportunities you'll have. Jesus took advantage of every event in His disciples' experience to teach them lessons about God. When the storm came up on the lake and threatened to sink the disciples' boat, or when evil men tried to trap Jesus by bringing an adulterous woman before Him, Jesus turned those situations into lessons for growth.

If you watch TV with your kids, you'll have many opportunities to discuss righteousness, moral living, sexual purity and other issues of the Christian life with your child. When you read with your child or help him with homework or school projects, you'll have opportunities to grow closer and impart lessons about character and diligence. Even times of conflict and tension can be teachable moments for growth and

We are not just trying to make our kids behave, we're also trying to make them Christlike. We're trying to mold and shape their character, attitude, faith and prayer life so that they resemble that of Jesus the Master.

instruction. Don't let those opportunities pass you by. Take advantage of each one.

Be Consistent and Dependable

Keep your promises so that your kids know they can count on you. When you must correct them, do so in reasonable and predictable ways: "I told you last time that if you did *A*, I would do *B*. And I am going to keep my word." Kids need to know that you will do what you say, whether you say you're going to take them to Walt Disney World on Saturday or you say you're going to ground them the next time they break curfew. Few things threaten a kid's security more than having a parent who is inconsistent. Say what you mean and do what you say.

Set Firm Limits

Kids need structure. They should have set times when homework must be done, a set bedtime, and set limits on television, computer games, and other entertainment activities. Make sure your kids do their schoolwork honestly and on time. Don't allow them to take unethical shortcuts, such as writing a book report based on a Cliff Notes summary, or copying another student's homework. Make sure your kids are aware that there's a cause-and-effect relationship between choices and consequences.

Alan, our youngest, is a good-hearted young man and fun to be around—but he's never cared for school. We had him in a small Christian school where he got a lot of individual attention, and he was just scraping by. But with the start of his junior year in high school, something went terribly wrong. We started getting phone calls about Alan's classroom behavior on a regular basis. It got to the point where just one call a day was a good day!

At first, it was a mystery. We couldn't figure out why Alan's deportment had taken such a nosedive, and he wouldn't explain it. But then Alan got caught in a fairly major issue, and we found out what caused the change in his behavior.

A new student had arrived that fall, and this kid made Eddie Haskell look like a saint! Though younger than Alan, this boy had a very strong personality and sucked Alan in like a Hoover. We cracked down hard, trying to get Alan to straighten up and fly right. We grounded him, took away his phone privileges, disallowed visits from friends—he even lost his job as a ball boy with the Orlando Magic! No matter what we did, nothing worked.

I believe we hold the all-time record for the grounding of a teenager— two years! Alan ended up being grounded throughout his junior and senior years of high school. These are the years when teenagers get their driver's license—and Alan was *not* allowed to drive! But no matter how we tightened the chokehold, his behavior didn't improve.

Alan was living proof of the biblical adage, "Bad company corrupts good character" (1 Cor. 15:33). Although we refused to surrender Alan to this other kid's influence, it was rough! We practically had to drag him across the finish line at his graduation ceremony. Although our main concern was Alan, we also prayed for his misguided friend and hoped the kid would get his act together.

I'm happy to report that, as I write these words, Alan is in his second full year since graduation. He now lives in southern California, near several of his brothers and sisters, and he's making his way in the world. We see a lot of good signs that Alan, as he nears age 20, is growing in his character. The best sign of all (and you could have peeled us off the carpet when this happened!) was when Alan called and asked us to send him sermon tapes from our church!

The point is this: Kids need limits and boundaries. It may seem that they don't respond when you impose consequences on their bad behavior. It may seem that they're never going to come around. But you still have to be the parent and maintain your rules and structure. Don't give up just because you don't see any change. Refuse to surrender and your perseverance will eventually pay off.

Never Discipline in Anger

When your children need correction, be consistent, be firm and be kind. If you are angry, give the kids—and yourself—some time out. Use that time to calm down, reflect and make a constructive decision about how to discipline your kids.

We tend to think that discipline equals punishment. In reality, the words "discipline" and "disciple" come from the same root word. Whenever we discipline our children, our goal should not be to punish them but to make disciples of them. If that is our view of discipline, it will transform the way we see our parenting role.

Be a Good Role Model

Whether you know it or not, your kids are watching your every move. They are learning what it means to be a good Christian and a good human being from watching how you live, how you make decisions, and how you respond in a crisis. As someone once said, our children will become what we are—so we'd better start becoming what we want them to be. If you are inconsistent, if you are a hypocrite, they'll be the first to know. So be a person of integrity. Be a good role model.

Praise Effort, Not Results

If your child doesn't perform as you had hoped, don't let your disappointment show. Always say, "I'm proud of you! You're a tough competitor! Awesome effort!" If you only praise a child when he succeeds, you convey that your love and acceptance are conditional. As dads, we want our kids to know that we are proud of them when they try hard, do their best, and give it all they've got—win or lose.

Treat Each Child as a Unique Personality

Jesus didn't treat Peter the same way He treated John. He had to take special measures with the impulsive Peter in order to teach him to rein in his volatile tendencies. Peter and John were distinct individuals; so are your kids. Each child is a unique individual with a personality unlike anyone else's. Disciple each of your children according to his or her uniqueness.

Forgive Your Kids

If you want to shape your kids to be Christlike disciples, then model the character of Jesus. Treat them as Jesus would. Forgive them, love them and restore them, just as Jesus forgave the Twelve and restored them to ministry even after they failed Him. Teach your kids what it means to follow Jesus by imitating Him yourself.

We sometimes forget how the world looks from our children's point of view. We forget that kids can't think and reason like grownups. They don't have grownup experience and they haven't reached a grownup level of development. By expecting too much of them, we shame them and make them feel smaller than they already are.

One of the most important jobs we have as dads is to build up our kids' confidence and competence by protecting them from feelings of shame and inadequacy. That means we need to stop and think before we say something like, "Why don't you use your head?" or "Give me that! I'll do it myself!" or "Can't you do anything right?" One of the worst things a divorced dad can say is, "You're just like your mother!" (Even a very small child can tell that's not a compliment.)

Shame is an acid that dissolves a human soul. I've talked to men in their forties, fifties and sixties who have said to me, "Of all the hurts I've had in my life, the worst were the things my dad said to me. I could never please that guy. He was always saying things that made me feel stupid and ashamed. I can remember some of the rotten things he said like it was yesterday."

You may be thinking, *I remember, too. My old man used to do that to me.* Okay, so now you remember what it feels like, right? You don't want to do that to your own kids, do you? You don't want their memories of you, 30 or 40 years from now, to be some hurtful comment that made them cringe in shame. If your dad said things like that to you, then it's time to break the cycle. It's time to stop tearing down your kids' self-confidence and start building them up to take on the world.

Be a warrior for your child's heart. Build your child up to be a warrior for God.

TEENAGERS: A DAD'S TOUGHEST CHALLENGE

The year 1996 was the year of my divorce. Not only was I a single parent during that year (the children lived with me), but get this: *Sixteen* of my kids were teenagers at the same time! During that year, the very hardest year of my life, I came to understand why some animals eat their young.

Sometimes it seems like a teenage boy is nothing but an iPod-toting space alien that oozes testosterone from its pores and continually asks for the car keys. And a teenage girl? Just a continuous loop of unintelligible chatter that wanders the mall with a cell phone stuck to the side of her head. Teenagers are a mystery—and having been a teenager back in some previous decade of the Dark Ages doesn't shed a single ray of light on what teenagers are about today. Our kids don't trust us, they don't think they have anything to learn from us, and it's almost impossible to get them to open up and tell us what's going on in their lives.

Yet, despite all the heartburn, ulcers and angina that teenagers cause, despite the fact that babies are cuter and puppies are more easily housebroken, teenagers do have their own special charm. Sometimes they'll surprise you and let you into their world, if only for a moment. Just when you're ready to give up on them, they'll show a flash of maturity or rationality, or they'll just say, "I love you, pop!" And for a moment, somewhere behind the nose ring, beneath the spiky hair, you'll catch a glimpse of the image of God. Just make sure that when that miraculous moment arrives, you're there to see it.

You may ask, "But what if my teenager is rebellious?" Hey, they're *all* rebellious! It's normal. The teen years are *supposed* to be years of rage and revolution. It's a time when kids think they are adults, and they want all the good stuff that goes along with being an adult—money, cars, freedom and (let's be candid) sex. But they aren't really adults, and they don't want the hard work and responsibility that also come with being an adult.

Because they are in that twilight zone between childhood and adulthood, they *need* to rebel against you and everything you stand for. It's part of a process psychologists call "individuation." For a while in the teen years, kids need to reject large parts of their upbringing, explore the ideas and values of the world around them, and decide for themselves what is real, what is right, what is true.

It may be hard to believe, but you should *want* them to rebel—to an extent. You should *want* them to individuate, to gradually separate themselves from you. If your teens show no signs of rebellion whatsoever, you should be concerned. One of two things might be going on, neither one of them healthy.

First, a completely nonrebelling teenager may simply feel repressed and controlled. He or she may not feel powerful enough or confident enough to take you on. Teens who never rebel at home are sometimes just marking time until they can get out from under their parents' scrutiny and authority. As soon as they are out of your sight—at a party, at summer camp, or away at college—they may jump at the chance to declare their independence in dangerous ways: wild partying, drinking, drugs, sex, and so forth. It's far better to give kids the freedom to harmlessly, safely rebel at home than to leave them no outlet for their rebellious impulses.

Second, a nonrebellious teenager may be an "approval addict," someone who has such a low sense of self-worth that he or she can only feel acceptable by continually pleasing others. As a Christian father, you shouldn't want to raise your kids to be insecure people-pleasers. You want them to be strong, confident—ready to fight for their dreams, faith and ideas.

So while it's true that teenage rebellion is a pain in the sacroiliac, a little rebellion is a good thing. In most cases, teen rebellion can't be avoided; you simply have to ride it out as best you can. If you've done your parenting job well, your teenagers will probably come through those rebellious years with their faith and values largely intact.

Of course, even when you've done all any parent can do, your teenagers may still reject your faith and values. Our kids are subjected to thousands of influences we aren't even aware of: peers, teachers, TV and movies, the music that screams in their headphones, the books and magazines they read, the things they pick up in Yahoo.com chat rooms or on MySpace.com blog pages. As influential as you are (and believe me, you do have a lot of influence with your teens!), you are still one

It may be hard to believe, but you should want your teenagers to rebel—to an extent. You should want them to individuate, to gradually separate themselves from you.

voice among hundreds that whisper or scream at your teens every day.

I know this is a scary time for you, Dad. I know it's hard to watch your teenagers make rebellious choices and treat your accumulated wisdom as a doormat to wipe their feet on. But look at it this way: Remember when you were their age. Remember some of the stupid and even dangerous things you did to rebel against your parents. You were a teenager once and you survived, didn't you? Keep praying, keep listening, and keep your cool. Odds are, you're all going to get through this. If I survived 16 teens at one time, believe me, you're gonna make it.

Here's a six-step plan for making a wise, godly, Asher-like response to your rebellious teenagers.

Step 1: Pick Your Battles with Care—and Prayer

Your kids will find many creative ways to rebel. Some ways will be relatively harmless—strange clothes, weird hair, a messy room, too much time on the phone, a bad attitude, pulling away from family activities. Others may be downright deadly, such as experimenting with drugs and sex or driving fast and recklessly. As a warrior in the Asher tradition, you continually have to ask yourself, *Should I ignore this—or clamp down? Is this the hill I want to die on?*

If a given form of rebellion is harmless, you probably ought to tolerate it—not like it, just tolerate it. Save your parental big guns for the larger issues, the risky or immoral behavior. If you give your kids a little room to safely rebel, they'll be less likely to defy your authority in more dangerous ways.

Step 2: Resist the Urge to Control Your Teen

It doesn't work; your teen can't be controlled. Worst of all, he or she knows it. When your teenager is rebelling and defying your authority, you'll feel an overwhelming temptation to resort to anger and punishment. With teens, anger and punishment tend to make things worse, not better.

I'm not saying that you should be permissive or passive when teens break the rules. They need to feel the consequences of poor choices. But you can impose consequences on your teen calmly and rationally, without controlling, without yelling. When your teenager tries to push your buttons, simply disconnect the anger circuit and remain firm, cool and controlled.

The mistake many frustrated parents make is saying, "You're going to do such and such." All the teenager has to do to gain the upper hand is to say, "No, I'm not." Solution: You, the parent, say, "If you do (or don't do) such and such, here's what will happen." Say it firmly but calmly, even sweetly (that drives 'em nuts!). You can even say, "I really don't want you to lose this privilege, but if you persist along this path, I *will* impose this consequence." Then, if the teenager persists, calmly carry out your promise. Take away the allowance, the computer, the cell phone, the car keys, the privilege.

Stop trying to force your kid to do this or that. You can't control his or her choices. But you *can* control *your* actions. And you can make your kid wish he or she had chosen more wisely.

Parenting teenagers is a balancing act. You have to learn to let go of them—but don't abandon them. You have to find ways of influencing them without trying to control them. You have to give them increasingly more permission without becoming permissive. They're on the verge of adulthood—but they haven't yet arrived. Teenagers are like kites: You want them to fly—but they can't fly high unless you hold on to that string. The trick is to keep reeling the string out, a little at a time, until they can soar on their own.

Step 3: Stay Cool and Stay Connected

Teenagers will say irrational things. They'll ridicule you as old-fashioned and narrow-minded even when you are patiently tolerating their ear-splitting screamo music and their retina-frying freakazoid hair. If you impose the most reasonable consequences (say, a week's grounding or suspended driving privileges), they'll accuse you of crimes against humanity and want to haul you before the World Court in The Hague.

Don't let it get to you. Remain calm. Teenagers are emotional, not rational. They are trying like all get-out to provoke you. Don't succumb to it. No matter what the disagreement is about or how loud and intense it becomes, keep telling them that you love them. Say, "I make these rules because I love you. I enforce these rules because I love you.

I know you wish I'd leave you alone and let you do whatever you please—and frankly, it would be easier on me to do that. But I love you too much to turn you loose. I'm going to hang in here with you and put up with your insults and yelling because I love you."

Sometimes your teens will push you away. They'll say, "I wish you'd just leave me alone! I wish you'd get out of my life!" That's a hurtful thing for a child to say and a painful thing for a dad to hear. You'll feel wounded by your child's rejection. You'll be tempted to say, "All right, if that's what you want, that's what you'll get." You'll feel like storming out of the room and slamming the door behind you. Don't do it.

Hang in there with your teens. They may say they want to be left alone, but on some deep level, every child fears abandonment. Even though they are reaching for adulthood, they still want to be connected to you. Even while they are pushing you away, they don't want to lose you completely. So tell your teens, "I'll take a step back if you want—but I'm still here and I'll always be here. Even when you say things to hurt me, I still love you and I'm not going to abandon you."

Step 4: Watch Your Tone of Voice

The way you speak has as much (or more!) effect on your kids as the words you use. The best way to talk to your kids is in a steady, firm, but kind voice. Avoid yelling, which scares kids. Also, avoid whining or pleading, which makes you sound weak and hungry for approval. Your voice should convey authority and self-control. Remember, the warrior within is always self-disciplined and under control.

Many people, particularly dads, have a tendency to raise their voices as conflict escalates. This suggests that you are losing control of the situation. Sometimes, the best way to deal with escalating conflict is by de-escalating your tone of voice. Instead of shouting over your kids, lower your voice so that they have to be quiet in order to hear you. Try it. If you're a shouter by nature, you'll be astonished at the results.

When you discipline your kids, keep it brief, keep it to the point (don't bring in all sorts of past issues and side issues), and avoid repeating yourself (unless your kids clearly didn't hear you the first time). Demonstrate that you are in control by being calm and polite, no matter how extreme and hysterical your child becomes.

Remember the last time you were stopped for speeding? The cop came to your window, politely called you "Sir," and when he was finished ruining your day, said, "Have a nice day." Why do the police act that way? Because they are trained to maintain a calm professionalism in confrontational situations. By doing so, they demonstrate that they are in control of the situation.

So take a lesson from the traffic cop. Be unfailingly polite and calm, no matter what your kids do. Show them who's in control and who's their daddy. Keep your emotions and your voice on the lowdown.

Step 5: In Times of Conflict, Focus on Your Faith

As your teenagers rebel, it's okay if they reject your political views or your taste in music and clothing. It's normal for them to challenge your authority and even question your intelligence. As Mark Twain once observed, "When I was a boy of fourteen, my father was so ignorant I could hardly stand to have the old man around. But when I got to be twenty-one, I was astonished at how much the old man had learned in seven years."

The greatest danger right now is that, while your teens are rebelling against your rules, your values and your authority, they may also reject your faith. They are on a journey of discovery, trying to decide what is real, true and important in their lives. They are being tugged out of your orbit by non-Christian friends and by the godless, hedonistic world around them. As they rebel against their earthly dad's authority, there's a danger that they may also reject the authority of God, their heavenly Father.

Unfortunately, the world around them has given your kids ample reason to reject God. As adults, we give them moral rules to live by, yet they look around them and see an immoral, godless and hypocritical adult world. They see that selfishness, greed and immorality are rewarded; integrity and character are punished. So they are cynical about morality and they question the credibility of adults to be role models for their lives.

More than ever before, you and I need to practice what we preach, or we lose the right to preach. We'd better make sure that we can truthfully tell our kids that Jesus is the Lord of our lives, that God is our Father, and that the Bible is the foundation of everything we do and say. When we fall short of that standard, we should admit it honestly and ask our kids to forgive us. If not, we give them every right to reject our faith.

It is said, "Nature abhors a vacuum." The same is true of human nature. If our kids reject our faith in Jesus Christ, they will be left with a spiritual vacuum—and it won't take them long to fill that spiritual vacuum with something else.

Many teenagers fill their spiritual vacuum with the occult—that is, with ouija boards, tarot cards, séances, astrology, fortune-telling, witchcraft (casting spells; sometimes called "wicca," "magick" or "white magic"), sorcery, channeling spirits, or satanism (worship of Satan or lesser devils). Some people think that such practices are just harmless superstition, like carrying a rabbit's foot for luck. But the Bible tells us that occult practices are dangerous to the soul and detestable to God:

> Let no one be found among you who sacrifices his son or daughter in the fire, who practices divination or sorcery, interprets omens, engages in witchcraft, or casts spells, or who is a medium or spiritist or who consults the dead. Anyone who does these things is detestable to the LORD (Deut. 18:10-12).

Teenagers often turn to occult practices because they feel powerless. Occultism holds out the appealing promise of secret powers that they can use to take control of their own lives. Teens who feel oppressed by parents and rejected by peers are especially vulnerable to the lure of the occult. Here are some ideas for safeguarding your kids against the occult.

First, teach your kids the biblical truth about spiritual forces. The Bible tells us that Christians are opposed by an evil intelligence called Satan (see Rev. 12:9), who leads a host of spiritual forces that seek to deceive and destroy us (see 1 Tim. 4:1; 1 Pet. 5:8). Our only defense against Satan is God's power, which we can call upon through prayer (see Eph. 6:11-16). Any spiritual power that doesn't come from God is from Satan and is to be avoided (see Gal. 1:8-9; 1 John 4:1).

Second, be aware of the cultural forces affecting your teenagers. Many of the influences that your teen is exposed to—music, TV, films, video games, computer games, books and Internet websites—are drenched in destructive spiritual messages. You have a responsibility to know what your teen is watching, listening to, and engaging in. Don't be passive or uninformed when your teens' souls are on the line.

Third, pray. If you know or suspect that your teens have become fascinated with dark spiritual forces, go to God and ask Him to protect their souls and to yank them out of the fire they are playing with: "Lord, in the name of Jesus, I ask you to shield my children's souls from the power and influence of the Evil One. Help my children to see the danger of dabbling with these powers that You have warned us against. Hold my children in Your loving hand and keep them out of the grip of Satan."

Fourth, if your teen has become mired in occult practices and you don't know what to do, get help. Talk to your pastor or the youth leader at your church. Ask for prayer, advice and help in reaching out to your teenagers and intervening in their lives.

Step 6: Whatever You Do, Don't Burn Your Bridges!

Don't ever give a teen an ultimatum like, "If you walk out that door, don't bother coming back!" Never do or say anything that would make your kids feel that your love is conditional or that if they cross a certain line, they can never return to you. Make sure your children know that you will always love and accept them, no matter what they have done or may do in the future.

Hurtful words, once spoken, can't be unsaid. You can apologize, you can ask forgiveness, but the things you say may lodge in your child's memory forever. Remember the example of the loving father and the prodigal son. The son insulted the father, implying, "I wish you were dead!" That son was as rebellious and disrespectful as a son could be—yet his loving father watched for him and welcomed him eagerly.

Hurtful words, once spoken, can't be unsaid. You can apologize, you can ask forgiveness, but the things you say may lodge in your child's memory forever.

Let me ask you a question: If someone were to offer you a genuine $10,000 bill, absolutely free and no strings attached, would you take it? I know I would, and I'm sure you would, too. Now, suppose that $10,000 bill had been in the gutter where it was stepped on, driven over and spattered with mud—would you still want it? Again, I would. Why? Because even though it was wrinkled, battered and covered with filth, that piece of paper would still be worth $10,000. Even if I had to slog through a pigsty to retrieve it, I would want that $10,000 bill, because underneath the stink and the muck, it's still worth as much as if it were crisp and fresh from the U.S. Mint.

Our teenagers are like that $10,000 bill. They may end up in life's gutter, where they get muddied, bloodied, spattered and spit on. In their immaturity and rebellion, they get into all kinds of muck and mire. Sometimes teenagers stink. But underneath all that teenage rebellion, there's infinite value. There's a soul worth saving, a life worth redeeming. All the wonderful promise you saw in that newborn is still in there in that teenager.

Do you know whose image is stamped on a $10,000 bill? Next time you open your wallet, take out a $10,000 bill and you'll see a picture of Salmon Portland Chase, Secretary of the Treasury under Abraham Lincoln. What's my point? Just this: There's an image stamped on your teenager, too—an infinitely more exalted image than that of Salmon P. Chase. It's the image of God the Father.

The next time you're on the verge of saying something you can never take back or are on the brink of burning the bridges of your father-child relationship, think of that $10,000 bill. Think about the image of God that's stamped on your teenager. Think about the eternal value hidden beneath that teenage muck and mire. The image of God may be hard to see in your child right now, but it's there. Your job, Dad, is to recover that image, shine it up, and bring it forth for the whole world to see.

The nation's foremost authority on child-rearing, Dr. James Dobson, once expressed how hard it is for anyone, including himself, to advise parents on raising teenagers. "Here's the distilled wisdom of all my research," he said. "Here is what you need to do if you have adolescents: Just get them through it! Just get them through it! Hang in there with them until the whitewater rapids of the teenage years are behind them."[2]

When people ask my advice on parenting teens, I always refer them to Psalm 127:3, where Solomon writes, "Sons are a heritage from the LORD, children a reward from him." Children aren't a dead weight that we're dragging through life. They're a reward! So I encourage parents to keep praying and loving their children, especially in those difficult teen years. I tell them, "Keep investing! Keep investing! Even though you don't see one flicker of hope or one sign of life, keep investing!"

I know it's hard to believe right now, but a day will come—somewhere on the other side of age 20—when your kids will emerge as real human beings. You may even get to hear them say, "Dad, you were right!" Or, "Dad, I was about to do something foolish, then I heard your voice in my head." Or, "Dad, you always taught us about this, and now I see what you mean." Or, best of all, "Dad, I love you so much!" Let me give you just a little taste of what you have to look forward to.

My son Bobby had spent five years as a baseball coach in the Cincinnati Reds farm system. In January 2005, the Washington Nationals (formerly the Montreal Expos) offered Bobby the chance to manage one of their farm clubs, the Vermont Expos in the New York-Penn League. Bobby accepted and, at the tender age of 27, became the youngest manager in organized baseball today.

After he stopped hyperventilating, Bobby called me with the news. Then he said, "Dad, what do I do now?"

As I write these words, Bobby's wrapping up his first season with the Vermont Expos, and it's been a baptism of fire. The team has racked up about twice as many losses as wins, and these games have been sheer agony for him. Bobby calls me after every game and tells me how it went, and then he asks my advice. It's been one of the most rewarding parenting experiences I've ever had—and it's taught me that fatherhood doesn't stop once your kid reaches the 18-year mark. It changes, and the father-son relationship has to take a different form once you're fellow adults. But the fathering doesn't stop.

Sometimes, after a really bad loss, I've had to scrape Bobby off the floor and say, "Bobby, you're gonna get through this. Right now, you've got a relief pitcher who's feeling even lower than you are, and you've got to put your arm around him and tell him you're going to put him right back in the next game, that you believe in him. That's leadership."

I've sat in the stands for over a dozen of Bobby's games. When I watch his team struggle, I suffer through the games right along with him. I can feel my heart quivering and my stomach puckering. I agonize over his games more than the Orlando Magic games. Why? Because Bobby's my son!

But you know what? I wouldn't want that agony to stop! I love being involved in Bobby's life this way. I love it that he calls me to report on his games and ask my advice. Every time we talk, I say, "Bobby, thank you for including me. Thank you for letting me participate in your life. Thank you for asking my advice. I'm not sure how many young people do that with their parents, and I'm grateful that you do."

Bobby recently sent me a note. When I opened it, several baseball cards fell out. The cards had Bobby's picture on them. The handwritten note read:

Believe me, I'm having my "frame guy" put something together to display my son's Expos cards! That's my payoff for investing in Bobby's teenage years. And let me tell you, I'm reaping a similar payoff in the lives of all my other kids as well.

So if you're a parent of teens, hang in there. Keep praying. Keep investing. A day will come when you'll know that you've raised a generation of spiritual descendents of Asher—heads of families, passing on the

Dad,

Here is my Expos card. Hope you like it. Thanks for being such a big part of my life, and thanks for being so interested in this season.

-Bobby

P.S. I sent a couple extra cards, if you want to have your frame guy put something together.

Asher tradition from one generation to another, and another, and another.

And you'll know it was worth it all.

Notes

1. Michael Reagan with Jim Denny, *Twice Adopted* (Nashville, TN: Broadman and Holman, 2004).
2. Dr. James Dobson, *Bringing Up Boys: Practical Advice and Encouragement for Those Shaping the Next Generation of Men* (Carol Stream, IL: Tyndale House Publishers, 2001).

DIMENSION 2:
CHARACTER

IMAGINE A MAN OF CHARACTER . . .

"Asher!" wailed Ijona, his wife. "Asher! He's gone! Ishvah's gone!"

Instantly awake, Asher jumped up from the mat he slept on. It was barely light outside. Looking around the room, he saw that Ijona was not in the house. Her cries had come from outside.

As he hurried toward the door, he looked at the mats where his children slept. Imnah, Ishvi, Beriah and Serah all stirred from their sleep. Ishvah's mat was empty—and his bow and arrows were gone as well.

Asher went outside and found Ijona standing by the stone cistern. Her hair fluttered in the chilly morning breeze. Her dark eyes frantically scanned the valley floor and the hillsides around the house. "Oh, Asher," she said, "he's run away!"

"He'll be back," Asher said unconvincingly. "Ishvah took his bow and went to do a little hunting before breakfast."

"No!" Ijona said, her voice rising in panic. "He ran away! He took the bow because he's not coming back!"

"You can't be sure—"

"I'm sure! I'm sure!" the mother insisted. "Don't you remember? I punished him last night for fighting with Arad."

"Ah. The metalsmith's son. I'd forgotten that he came home yesterday with a bloody nose."

"I told him he couldn't leave our yard for two days," Ijona said, wringing her hands. "He seemed so angry when he went to bed last night. This morning, I got up before dawn and he'd already gone. He knows he's not to leave, so he must have run away!"

Asher nodded. It certainly looked that way.

Ishvah was his young Warrior, and he had taken his bow—the bow Asher himself had made for Ishvah as a birthday present. It was a beautiful longbow, made of hardwood, ox horn and sinew, with a handgrip that Asher had carved himself. He had taught Ishvah to make his own arrows, fletch them with feathers, and tip them with flint or bronze.

Asher looked at the ground.

"What are you doing?" Ijona asked tearfully, brushing the wind-blown hair from her eyes.

"Looking for footprints. I'm going to track him."

"Take Imnah with you. He can help—"

"No," Asher said firmly. "I can go faster alone. . . . His tracks are old. The boy must have left in the middle of the night. I'll have to hurry."

Asher went back to the house, strapped his hunting knife to his hip, and took a pouch of dried meat for his journey. Then he kissed Ijona at the door and walked away.

He followed the tracks along a little path that led west into the olive grove and through a little saddle between two hills. *Strange*, Asher thought. *If Ishvah doesn't want to be found, why is he keeping to the path? He knows how to cover his tracks. He made no effort to hide where he's going.*

The sun climbed the eastern sky, warming Asher's back as he hurried along the path. It was past mid-morning when he topped a low, grassy rise and looked down the path to see—

"Ishvah!" Asher whispered.

The boy was about 50 yards away, trudging toward him, head lowered, shoulders sagging, looking totally forlorn. Ishvah didn't see Asher at first. So Asher called loudly—

"Ishvah! Ishvah, my son!"

The boy stopped in surprise—and then ran to his father as fast as he could. "Father!" he called, sobbing. "Father! I'm so sorry!"

Ishvah ran into his father's arms.

Asher's arms enfolded the boy—and then he realized something was wrong. The beautiful bow that should have been slung over Ishvah's back was gone. So was the quiver of arrows.

Asher held Ishvah at arm's length and looked into his eyes. "My son," he said, "where is your bow? Where are your arrows?"

Ishvah looked down. He couldn't meet his father's eyes. "I'm sorry, Father," he said. "I— I gave the bow to Arad. I told him to keep it. The arrows, too." Tears spilled down the boy's cheeks.

"Why? I made that bow for you. I thought you loved it."

"I do, Father," Ishvah said miserably.

"Then why—"

"Arad's my friend. When we fought yesterday, he said things that made me angry. He called me a baby! He called me a coward! He laughed at me! It made me so mad, I felt my blood boiling inside of me. So I jumped on him and hit him. When I was finished hitting him, his nose was bloody— I think I broke it. His eye was turning black and swollen shut. And I saw him spit one of his teeth in the dust. He was crying, Father, and he told me he hated me, and he never wanted to see me again."

"What about your bloody nose?" Asher said. "Arad hurt you, too."

"A little blood," Ishvah said. "That's nothing. But I hurt him a lot."

"Yes," Asher said, "I suppose you did."

"I came home last night and went to bed, but I couldn't sleep. All I could think of was that I'd hurt my best friend, and I'd made him hate me. I got up in the middle of the night and I walked to Arad's house. When he came out this morning, I called to him and told him I was sorry."

"And you gave him your bow."

The boy hung his head. "Yes," he said. "I didn't want to lose it—but I didn't have anything else to give him to show him how bad I felt for hurting him. I'm sorry, Father."

"You're sorry? For what?"

"For giving away the bow. For disappointing you."

Asher smiled and his eyes glistened. He pulled his boy to chest and embraced him tightly. "You didn't disappoint me, Ishvah," he said in a husky voice. "You made me proud."

Ishvah's eyes widened. "How did I make you proud?"

Asher clapped his son on the back. "Someday I'll explain it to you. Come on, Ishvah, let's go home. Your mother is worried about you."

That day, Ishvah ceased to be a boy. He became a man—a choice young man, a man of character.

Be a "Choice Man" of Character

In February 1965, I loaded up my car and drove to Spartanburg, South Carolina, home of the Spartanburg Phillies. At 24, I was about to become one of the youngest general managers in the history of professional sports. I was also on my way to meet a man who would change my life—the team owner, Mr. R. E. Littlejohn.

When I arrived in Spartanburg, Mr. Littlejohn was not home, but his wife invited me in. She offered me refreshments and then sat down and told me all about her husband, whom she called "Mister R. E." I was struck by the genuine admiration in her voice as she said, "You'll never meet another man like Mister R. E. He's the greatest man in the world." After I got to know Mr. R. E. Littlejohn, I totally agreed.

I met Mr. Littlejohn in his office the following day. He was a refined, soft-spoken Southern gentleman who took a genuine interest in everyone he met. I couldn't put my finger on just what made him so special, but whatever it was, I admired it—and I wanted to have those same qualities in my own life.

Mister R. E. explained my duties as general manager: fix up the rundown ballpark, promote baseball and build attendance at the games, and sell advertising in the game programs. He knew I was young and green, but he never second-guessed me, never criticized me, never told me how to do my job. He praised my accomplishments and never criticized my mistakes. He seemed content to let me learn by trial and error. I knew he wanted me to succeed, and I grew to love him like a father.

I have never worked harder in my life than I did when I worked for Mister R. E. I wasn't afraid of him—I couldn't have had a more kind and patient boss. But I was afraid of failure. That fear drove me to work from dawn to dusk, seven days a week. I had no social life. I didn't know the first thing about delegating, so I did everything myself, from selling advertising space to cleaning restrooms to painting the outfield walls.

My efforts paid off. When the season opened, attendance at the ballpark soared. The people who came had a great time, not only at the games but also at our pre-game promotional events. The entire city of Spartanburg sat up and took notice. I was a success!

Yet I felt restless, empty and dissatisfied—and I couldn't figure out why! I got rave reviews, made good money, drove a big car, and got nods of approval from the leading citizens of the town. Why wasn't I happy?

God wasn't part of my life in those days. In fact, the only time God ever came to mind was when I talked to Mister R. E. He had a deep Christian faith that he spoke of often. To me, Mister R. E. exemplified what it means to be a Christian—yet I couldn't put my finger on what it was about him that reminded me so much of Jesus.

One day, I told him, "I'll bet Jesus Christ must've been a lot like you."

I meant it as a compliment, but he looked at me as if I had uttered the unutterable! "Pat," he said softly, "no man can compare with the Lord Jesus."

I didn't understand how I had offended him. But the fact that he had responded with such humility made me admire him all the more.

What was it about Mister R. E. that was so impressive? What did he have that I didn't have? I was honest and hardworking and I didn't drink or smoke. I thought I was a decent person.

Yet there was something about Mister R. E. that went far beyond being "decent." I kept hearing the words of Mrs. Littlejohn: "You'll never meet another man like Mister R. E."

In February 1968, I went to a folk music concert at the Spartanburg auditorium. The folk group sounded a lot like Peter, Paul and Mary or the New Christy Minstrels. At one point, they put down their guitars and talked to the audience about having a relationship with Jesus Christ.

After the concert, I hung around and struck up a conversation with a petite blonde singer in the group. Fact is, I made a play for her, but she adroitly fended it off. She gave me a little booklet to read, and then said goodnight and walked away. I stuck the booklet in my pocket, realizing that the blonde folk singer had the same inner quality that I saw in

Mister R. E. Littlejohn—a joy, a Christlike radiance. I wanted that in my own life.

Back at my apartment, I took out the booklet and examined it. The title was *Have You Heard of the Four Spiritual Laws?* I flipped it open and read:

Law One: God loves you and has a wonderful plan for your life.

Law Two: Man is sinful and separated from God. Therefore, he cannot know and experience God's love and plan for his life.

Law Three: Jesus Christ is God's only provision for man's sin. Through Him you can know and experience God's love and plan for your life.

Law Four: We must individually receive Jesus Christ as Savior and Lord, and then we can know and experience God's love and plan for our lives.

I didn't sleep well that night. I got up the next morning with my mind whirling with questions.

I tried to immerse myself in my work. I made a few sales calls, but I couldn't concentrate. All I could think of was how empty I felt. I went to my office at the ballpark and paced like a caged tiger. I couldn't work or even think. Finally, at around three in the afternoon, I got in my car and drove over to see Mister R. E.

In his office, I told him what I'd been going through. I told him about the concert, my conversation with the blonde folk singer, The Four Spiritual Laws, everything. As I told him, he said, "Pat, that's wonderful!"

"What's wonderful about it? I'm miserable!"

"Don't you see?" Mister R. E. said. "My wife and I have been praying for you ever since you came to Spartanburg. Now you're ready to make a decision for Christ. Pat, now's the time."

It was true. I was ready. It was time. That's why I had come to talk to Mister R. E. I wanted him to tell me how I could begin living for Jesus Christ.

Suddenly, I understood what the Four Spiritual Laws were saying to me—that God loved me and wanted to fill up my empty life with His love. I understood that I was a sinner and that Jesus had taken all the punishment for my sin so that I could live forever with Him.

So at quarter of four on February 22, 1968, I surrendered. My struggle was over. Jesus had won—but I had won, too!

From that day forward, I understood that elusive "something" I had sensed in Mr. R. E. Littlejohn. I understood why I had looked at him and thought I had glimpsed Christ. It was because Mr. R. E. Littlejohn was a man of Christlike character. He was the kind of man Asher would have called a "choice man," a man whose way of life was a testimony to others because the character of Jesus shone through everything he did and said.

THE TRAITS OF A "CHOICE MAN"

"All these were descendants of Asher," 1 Chronicles 7:40 tells us, "heads of families, *choice men*, brave warriors and outstanding leaders" (emphasis added). What makes a man stand out as a choice man by Asher's standards? Just one thing: good character.

I would define "character" as "an ingrained pattern of qualities, traits and moral attributes that define how a person will act in times of stress, crisis or temptation." For example, a choice man has the character trait of *honesty*. That means he will not lie, even if he must pay a price to tell the truth. He will not steal, even if his need is great. He will not cut ethical corners, even if he is severely tempted and no one would ever know the difference.

A choice man says "I accept responsibility" instead of "It wasn't my fault." A choice man programs himself to do the right thing, not the easy thing. A choice man can be relied upon as moral, ethical, principled and godly, whether in public or in private, whether his behavior is witnessed by thousands or he is alone and unobserved.

What makes a man stand out as a choice man by Asher's standards? Just one thing: good character.

I was visiting with Alvin Dark, the longtime major league shortstop and manager. He told me that his son was having a rough time in life and that he was not always making very good decisions. Incidentally, Alvin is approaching his mid-eighties, so his son is not a kid. Alvin said to his son, "Why do you think you keep making poor choices in life?"

"Dad," his son said, "I just don't have any character."

"Oh, yes, you do," Alvin said. "Do what's right and you'll develop character. A man knows what's right and what's wrong."

Here are some of the character qualities of a choice man like Asher and his descendents.

Integrity

To have integrity is to be a whole and integrated person—no masks, no duplicity, no chinks in the armor. The word "integrity" comes from the Latin *integritas*, meaning "soundness," which comes from *integer*, meaning "whole, complete." When our nation went from racial segregation to racial integration, our society became meshed into a unified whole—and our nation, at last, had integrity.

If you have integrity as a man of God, it means you are the same man at home, at work and at church. You don't pretend to be a man of honor and truth at church on Sunday mornings and then cut corners and cut throats out in the business world the rest of the week.

Integrity is essential to trust. If people know that you are a man of integrity, they'll depend on you and look to you as a leader. You'll have a good reputation: "He's no empty suit. He's the real deal."

On July 3, 1775, at Cambridge, Massachusetts, General George Washington took command of the Continental Army—17,000 untrained, undisciplined and poorly organized short-term militiamen from throughout the 13 colonies. To his dismay, he found that there was not enough gunpowder and ammunition for his troops. Washington knew that his army lacked the training and equipment to wage a successful war against the superior British forces. How, then, did he hope to win? By building an army of integrity.

As he stood under a tall elm tree, General Washington delivered a short but stirring speech to his troops. He concluded with these words from Psalm 101:7—"No one who practices deceit will dwell in my house; no one who speaks falsely will stand in my presence." Commanding an army of integrity, General Washington waged six years of war—and he founded a nation.

Franklin Graham was once asked how his father, Dr. Billy Graham, had maintained his influence for God through six decades of ministry. The younger Graham replied that his father's integrity made the difference. "The Billy Graham you see in public," he said, "is the same Billy Graham we children have seen at home. I've been around people in the public eye who turn into different people when the cameras turn off. That's not the case with my father."

It's true. In fact, a journalist in London once confided to an executive of the Billy Graham Evangelistic Association, "We have searched for any trash we could find in Billy Graham's life so we could do an exposé. We couldn't find a thing, so we just gave up digging."

When my son Michael was 19, I had a conversation with him over lunch. As we talked, he used the word "integrity." So I said, "Tell me, Mike, what is your definition of integrity?"

He thought for a moment, and I could see the wheels turning. Then he said, "Integrity is honesty with a little oomph."

I laughed. "Mike," I said, "you nailed it, pal."

Today, some say that integrity doesn't matter. Some even seem to admire the man who lies, cheats, steals and gets away with it. They admire a man who is able to compartmentalize, to segment his life into various compartments: "Isn't he amazing? He can lie and cheat in his personal life and still be a great leader!"

Well, go ahead if you like—buy a used car from that man, vote for him, let him date your daughter. But I won't. I want nothing to do with a compartmentalized man. If he'll steal from others, eventually he'll get around to stealing from me. I don't intend to give him the opportunity. I choose to deal with men of integrity, choice men like Asher.

Honesty

The character quality of honesty can be defined as "uncompromising truthfulness and incorruptibility." A choice man of honesty not only tells the truth but also owns up to his mistakes ("That was my fault"), reports all his taxes to the government, buys his own office supplies instead of "borrowing" them from work, and has no bootlegged software or music files on his computer.

Success in business is built on honesty. Cheat a customer once and you've lost that customer forever. Most people today are willing to pay a little more to deal with someone they can trust. Earl Nightingale, cofounder of the Nightingale-Conant audio-video-publishing empire, put it this way: "If honesty did not exist, it would have to be invented as it is the surest way of getting rich."

We've all heard the story of how, in his boyhood, George Washington chopped down a cherry tree. When confronted by his father, the boy instantly confessed, "I cannot tell a lie. I did it with my little hatchet." No one knows how much historical fact (if any) there is in that story, but we do know that it first appeared in a book by Parson Mason Weems, *The Life of Washington*. We also know that the story made a big impact on a young Abraham Lincoln.

When Lincoln was a boy, he borrowed a copy of Weems's *The Life of Washington* from a neighboring farmer. Each night, the boy read from the book by lamplight and then placed it in a hollow space between two logs in the wall of his cabin. He thought the book would be safe there, but one night it rained and water leaked through, soaking the book. The next morning, young Lincoln found the book stained and warped.

He took the ruined book back to the man from whom he had borrowed it. "I meant to take good care of it, sir," he said, "but I let it get ruined by the rain. I haven't any money to pay for it, so I came here to ask what you'd have me to do make it right."

The farmer said, "Come to my farm and shuck corn for three days. That'll pay for the book, and you can keep it."

Young Abe Lincoln couldn't believe his good fortune! All he had to do was shuck corn for three days and the book was his to keep! The incident taught young Lincoln the rewards of honesty and helped earn him the nickname "Honest Abe."

Once, when Lincoln worked as a clerk at a general store, he discovered that he had overcharged a customer by a few cents. So he closed the store and walked to the customer's home, which was several miles away, and paid the few pennies that were due. On a different occasion, Lincoln discovered that his weighing scales were improperly balanced, causing his customers to be cheated by an ounce or two. So he weighed out a few ounces of tea and took it to a lady whose tea purchase had been shorted the previous day—much to the lady's surprise.

Other stories of Lincoln's uncompromising honesty came from his years as a poor but honest lawyer. Lincoln once accepted a case brought to him by a mentally challenged young woman. A con man had cheated her out of some property. Lincoln and his law partner agreed on a fee ahead of time, based on the expectation that the trial would take a certain number of days to litigate. In fact, the trial lasted only 15 minutes and the property was returned to the young woman. Lincoln's partner was gleeful over earning a big fee for 15 minutes' work. Lincoln insisted on returning his share of the fee to the young woman, saying, "I'd rather starve than swindle her."

Honest Abe Lincoln was a choice man in the Asher mold.

Diligence

A diligent man is a hard worker and a self-starter with an uncompromising commitment to excellence. The Christian virtue of diligence can be found throughout the Old and New Testaments. In the book of Genesis, we see that work was originally intended to be a good thing for humanity. Genesis 2:15 tells us that God "took the man and put him in the Garden of Eden to work it and take care of it." It was only after the Fall, when Adam and Even broke God's commandment, that work turned into back-breaking drudgery.

"Lazy hands make a man poor, but diligent hands bring wealth," says Proverbs 10:4. And in Ecclesiastes 9:10 we are told, "Whatever your hand finds to do, do it with all your might." Similar counsel runs throughout the New Testament. For example, Paul writes, "Whatever you do, work at it with all your heart, as working for the Lord, not for men. . . . It is the Lord Christ you are serving" (Col. 3:23-24).

In June 2005, I was in Washington, D.C., and I hired a tour guide who took me on a four-hour walking excursion. It was a hot, humid day in our nation's capital, so I stopped at a little beverage stand to buy some bottled water. I struck up a conversation with a Vietnamese woman who ran the stand. In heavily accented English, she said, "America is the greatest country on Earth! If you work hard, you can accomplish anything you want!"

That's an attitude we should all have. Choice men don't simply see hard work as a key to success (although it is). They see diligence as a moral imperative. Laziness and sloppiness are sins in the eyes of choice men in the Asher mold.

Humility

To be a choice man of humility means maintaining a sober view of oneself and others. Humility doesn't mean having a low opinion of oneself. Those who continually run themselves down are often the least humble of all. Saying "I'm wretched" or "I'm worthless" or "I'm nothing" is just their way of getting attention!

Genuine humility is a strength, not a weakness. A choice man of humility is confident without being arrogant. He respects himself without tearing others down. He doesn't let other people determine his sense of self-worth. His ego can't be inflated by flattery, nor deflated by insults. Mother Teresa once put it this way: "If you are humble nothing can touch you, neither praise nor disgrace, because you know who you are."

Patience

A choice man of Asher-like character is willing to defer immediate gratification in order to achieve future benefits. Patience is the ability to be at peace while waiting. In this age of fast food, microwave ovens, and high-speed Internet, we are no longer willing to wait, to endure, to hope, to expect. But choice men are men of patience. It's a character quality

A choice man of Asher-like character is willing to defer immediate gratification in order to achieve future benefits. Choice men are men of patience.

that I confess I've had to learn the hard way.

A number of years ago, I flew from Orlando to Michigan to give a speech at the Ford Motor Company in Dearborn. A limo driver was supposed to meet me at the airport. I waited an hour, and then got another ride to the hotel.

Arriving at the front desk, I saw that the desk clerk was being trained while helping the customer ahead of me. It was an agonizingly slow process, and I was impatient. I paced, fumed and sighed loudly. The clerk knew I was upset, and that didn't enhance his efficiency one bit.

Finally, the clerk finished with the man ahead of me and I stepped up to the desk. "Just a moment, sir," the clerk said. Then he left. I couldn't believe it! He left!

Just then, the man who had registered ahead of me stopped and said in a soft tone, "You know, it's not the clerk's fault. This is his first day on the job and he's doing the best he can. All your huffing and puffing sure won't make him go any faster."

I felt like hiding behind a potted palm. The guy was right. Before I could think of a reply, he stepped into the elevator. The thought hit me: *Oh, no! What if he's in the audience for my speech tomorrow?* When the clerk returned, I took extra pains to be kind and patient.

The next morning, I left my room and got into the elevator. Wouldn't you know it? There was my friend from the night before—the fellow who had gently lectured me on the value of patience.

I immediately apologized for my behavior. "You're right," I said. "My behavior last night was inexcusable." We chatted until the elevator reached the lobby, and then he went left and I went right. I was relieved that he wouldn't be in the room while I gave my talk! I'd come to *give* a lecture; instead, I *got* a lecture on the value of patience.

Former UCLA basketball coach John Wooden used to tell his players, "Be quick, but don't hurry." A choice man like Asher knows that patience is a virtue.

Self-discipline

A choice man of good character is one who has mastered his impulses and behavior. He's not a slave to drinking, smoking, drug abuse, over-eating, gambling or sexual compulsions (such as adultery or an addiction to pornography). A self-disciplined man knows how to manage his time well. He maintains a healthy, balanced lifestyle, allowing adequate time for exercise, rest and devotional time with God.

Phil Jackson, head coach of the Los Angeles Lakers, told me a story from his senior year at the University of North Dakota. "My coach was Bill Fitch," he said. "I was captain of the team, but at one point I had the job taken away from me. We were playing a game in Chicago, and I went out with some friends to Rush Street. I got back to the hotel after curfew, so Bill took away my captaincy. He said, 'You won't be captain again until you prove you deserve it.' Bill made me prove to him that I had the self-discipline to lead the team. In time, I earned my job back and we went on to a successful season. Bill gave me a lesson in discipline that has helped me throughout my life."

CHARACTER UNDER CONSTRUCTION

You can't lead anyone where you will not go. You can't influence a generation of choice men if you are not a man of character yourself. If you want to raise children and grandchildren of integrity, you must model it to them—especially at times when you think no one is watching. Though our kids aren't very good at listening to what we say, they watch what we do!

"But," you may ask, "isn't there any time when I can take a break? Couldn't I let my hair down, get a little wild, and just make sure no one knows?" No way! You either have good character or you don't. It's not something you turn on and off like a light switch. If you don't have character when nobody's looking, you don't have it at all.

"But what if I make a mistake?" you may ask. "What if I blow it and disappoint the very people I'm trying to influence?" What do you mean, "if"? You *will* blow it! We're fallen people living in a fallen world, and you *will* slip up, guaranteed. That doesn't mean you can never be a choice man again. True, sin is serious, and it has consequences—don't ever diminish the awfulness of sin! But when you sin, you still have an opportunity to demonstrate character. You can set an example of honesty

("I sinned") and humility ("Please forgive me").

That's what choice men do. When you fall, take it like a man. Admit your sin, repent of it, and then get back on your feet and keep going. That's the counsel of the psalmist David: "Then I acknowledged my sin to you and did not cover up my iniquity. I said, 'I will confess my transgressions to the Lord'—and you forgave the guilt of my sin" (Ps. 32:5). And that's what James tells us: "Therefore confess your sins to each other and pray for each other so that you may be healed" (Jas. 5:16).

We are always under construction. We never stop building our character. Throughout our lives, every decision we make leads either to stronger character or to a weakening of the foundation of our souls. No man can ever rise higher than the limits of his character. So if we want to keep growing as men and as followers of Christ, we have to keep building and extending the limits of our character.

There's not much that you and I can do to make ourselves more talented or more intelligent. But even if we can't increase our talent or our brain power, we can always enlarge our character. We can actually *choose* the character we will have! We strengthen our character by the choices we make every day.

And remember this: A seemingly small and insignificant choice can lead to unimaginable destruction and devastation in our lives. The greatest example of this principle is the story of King David and his sin with Bathsheba. It all started with a small choice on David's part. In 2 Samuel 11, we read:

> In the spring, at the time when kings go off to war, David sent Joab out with the king's men and the whole Israelite army. . . . But David remained in Jerusalem. One evening David got up from his bed and walked around on the roof of the palace. From the roof he saw a woman bathing. The woman was very beautiful (vv. 1-2).

At a time when kings go off to war, King David stayed behind in Jerusalem. David was not where he was supposed to be, and he was not doing what he was supposed to be doing. His job was to be a warrior— but he neglected his calling. So he had time on his hands. He went up on the roof of his palace and saw a woman bathing. He was doing what all too many of us are prone to do, with the aid of cable TV or the Internet: David was engaging in voyeurism.

He probably told himself, *What's the harm in looking? Every man looks. Guys are just wired that way. It's just a little porn—and she's really hot.* But it didn't end there. It never does.

David couldn't stop thinking about the woman. He had already compromised his integrity by looking. Now he proceeded on to lusting. He sent messengers out to bring the woman to him. She came and he had sex with her. Even though King David knew that the woman, Bathsheba, was married to Uriah, one of the loyal warriors in his army, he knowingly took her and committed adultery.

When Bathsheba became pregnant, King David realized that he had to cover up his adultery with the sin of deception. So he called Uriah home from the battlefield and tried to coax the man into sleeping with Bathsheba. But Uriah, being a choice man of loyalty, faithfulness and integrity, refused to indulge in the pleasures of his own marriage bed as long as his soldiers were camped out on the battlefield. David's attempted cover-up failed. He would have to do something more extreme.

Like murder.

So King David sent Uriah back to the battlefield, had him placed on the front lines in the thick of the battle, and then ordered the other men to withdraw so that Uriah would be slaughtered by the enemy. It worked. Uriah was killed, and David took Bathsheba as his wife.

"But," the Scriptures tell us, "the thing David had done displeased the Lord" (2 Sam. 11:27). God led the prophet Nathan to confront David with his sin. David repented and God forgave him, but the natural consequences of David's sin haunted him throughout the rest of his life. David paid an incredibly high price for his lapse of character.

Character is not something you turn on and off like a light switch. If you don't have character when nobody's looking, you don't have it at all.

It started with just a little crack in David's integrity, a seemingly small choice. As you and I so often do, he turned his back on the warrior within; he went up on the rooftop instead of out onto the battlefields of life. He was not where he was supposed to be and not doing what he was supposed to be doing—and he looked at what he shouldn't have been seeing. From that point on, it was just a steady downhill slide toward adultery, murder, shame and brokenness.

This is not just a time-worn story from an ancient book. This is a principle of life that's as valid today as it ever was. Some years ago, a Christian television host seemed to have it all. His religious talk show was carried 24/7 on a satellite network that he had built. He also operated a successful theme park. Contributions to his nonprofit corporation were estimated at a million dollars per week. It all collapsed in scandal when the news broke that he'd been paying hush money to a woman with whom he'd had an adulterous affair.

After he was convicted and sentenced to federal prison, this man recalled, "Ninety-five percent of my life was in order, but five percent of my life was concealed and I never turned that part of my life over to God. That five percent is what brought me down."

In Psalm 15:1 (*NASB*), the Psalmist David asked the question, "O LORD, who may abide in Your tent? Who may dwell on Your holy hill?" Then David answered his own question with a description of a choice man after the example of Asher: "He who walks with integrity, and works righteousness, and speaks truth in his heart" (v. 2, *NASB*).

As I was writing this book, I saw Billy Graham's daughter, Anne Graham Lotz, on the Fox News Channel's *Hannity & Colmes* show. She said that Dr. Graham's three-day crusade in New York City, June 2005, was her father's last and that he was at peace with that. She said that, at 86, her father had lost much of his hearing and her mother, Ruth Bell Graham, was blind and unable to walk. But their minds are sharp and they enjoy being together at home.

Co-host Alan Colmes said that he felt privileged to have been at the New York crusade and to have met Dr. Graham. "I've never seen a clearer pair of eyes," Colmes recalled. "They penetrate into your very being."

"Daddy has nothing to hide," Anne said in reply. "His eyes are clear because his character is solid."

May the same be true of you and me. May we be true and godly warriors. May our eyes be clear and our character solid because we are choice men of God.

Build a Generation of "Choice People"

On May 27, 1974, I discovered what it truly means to worship God. That was the day I witnessed the birth of my first child. When that baby boy was born strong, pink and healthy, I looked heavenward and praised God.

We named our son after my two fathers—my birth father, Jim Williams, and my spiritual father, Mr. R. E. Littlejohn, who led me to the Lord. I was general manager of the Atlanta Hawks at the time, and James Littlejohn Williams was born on the day of the NBA draft. So I decided to get Jimmy off to a good start in pro sports. I tried to draft him straight from the delivery room into the NBA.

In the tenth round of the draft, as all the executives from around the league were listening via conference phones, I announced, "The Atlanta Hawks select James Williams!"

"James Williams?" a voice cut in. "You mean Fly?"

Jim "Fly" Williams was a junior at Austin Peay State University in Clarksville, Tennessee. Drafting him would have been a rules violation.

"No," I said. "James Littlejohn Williams."

"What school?" asked Si Gourdine, assistant to the commissioner.

"Piedmont Hospital in Atlanta," I said. "He's nineteen and a half inches tall, seven and a half pounds."

Three ticks passed in stunned silence.

Then Si Gourdine deadpanned, "Disallowed."

Three years later, we were expecting a second child. On the night before the NBA draft, I was at Temple University, where a game was about to begin. I was walking at the end of the court, just behind the basket, when I heard a phone ring. The phone was inside a box on the support post behind the basket. Curious, I opened the box and answered the phone.

It was my wife!

What are the odds that she would call the Temple University basketball arena, trying to locate me, and that I would just happen to answer the phone? Is that a God-thing or what?

"The baby's coming," she said. "It's time to go to the hospital."

"I'm on my way!"

At 11:30 the next morning, June 10, 1977, Bobby Williams was born—exactly 90 minutes before the NBA draft was due to begin. Again, I ask you: What are the odds? My first two sons were both born on the day of the NBA draft.

Two years later, on July 28, 1979, our third child (and first daughter) Karyn came into the world. With Karyn, as with Jimmy and Bobby, the miracle of childbirth was a worship experience for me.

After Karyn's birth, we adopted two daughters from South Korea, Andrea Michelle and Sarah Elizabeth. That's when I discovered that no matter how your children arrive, whether by the Lamaze method or by Northwest Airlines, a child is a miraculous gift from God.

On June 12, 1984, just five months after we received Andrea and Sarah into our home, our third son was born. We named him Michael Patrick after Phillies slugger Mike Schmidt and me.

Although Mike was the last of our birth children, we continued to make room in our home for more kids: Thomas, Stephen, David, Peter, Brian, Sammy, Gabriella, Katarina, Richie, Daniela, Alan and Caroline. They came from South Korea, the Philippines, Romania and Brazil.

Very early in the process of building this megafamily of ours, I was struck by an awesome realization: I was taking on a staggering responsibility. That responsibility was the same whether we were bringing kids into the world by birth or flying kids into our home from all around the world. My task, for the next few decades, was to train a houseful of little sin-prone, fallen descendents of Adam and Eve to become choice men and choice women of Christlike character.

It was the same challenge that confronted Asher when he looked around at the faces of his sons Imnah, Ishvah, Ishvi and Beriah and of his daughter, Serah. The only difference was that Asher only had five kids to worry about. I had *18*—make that 19 after my remarriage.

RAISING CHOICE KIDS

In the previous chapter, we looked at some of the character qualities we need to be choice men of God. These character qualities include integrity, honesty, diligence, humility, patience and self-discipline. Now let's look at some additional character traits and at ways to instill these traits in our kids.

Responsibility

The character trait of responsibility is an ingrained tendency to act productively, reliably and decisively. Responsible people don't wait for someone to tell them what to do; they see what needs to be done and they do it. Responsible people don't need constant monitoring or reminding. They admit and correct their own mistakes—no excuses. There are several ways we build the character trait of responsibility in our kids:

- *Assign age-appropriate tasks and goals to them.* Monitor their progress but *don't interfere.* Allow them to succeed or fail on their own. When they fail, talk to them about the lessons they can learn from their failure.
- *Affirm your kids when they act responsibly.* When they take responsibility for mistakes or perform a task without being nagged, clap 'em on the back and say, "I'm proud of the way you accept responsibility!"
- *Avoid bribing a child with money or other tangible rewards.* A genuinely responsible young person should want to be responsible purely for the good feeling that comes with doing the right thing—not for the sake of getting paid. If you want to build a sense of responsibility in your kids, words of affirmation are payment enough.

The best way to build the trait of perseverance is by assigning tasks and challenges that demand a sustained effort over a period of time.

Perseverance

Nothing worthwhile is ever achieved easily or quickly. The world needs choice young men and choice young women who will persevere through obstacles, setbacks and opposition. Where do we find such young people? We train them!

The best way to build the trait of perseverance is by assigning tasks and challenges that demand a sustained effort over a period of time. We should teach our kids that good things come to those who persevere. When they encounter obstacles and want to quit, we become cheerleaders: "C'mon, you can't quit now! You're doing great! You're gonna make it!"

When your kids finally complete that project or task, it's time to celebrate! Make sure they are rewarded for persevering to the end—not with money or material stuff, but with a warm sense of accomplishment and your big smile of parental pride. Sure, perseverance has its tangible rewards, but let those come as a natural consequence of your kids' accomplishments. As you celebrate your kids' achievements, you'll see them become unstoppable and unsinkable.

Speaking of unsinkable, let me tell you a story about four of the Williams boys. In November 1988, we adopted four Filipino brothers, ages nine, eight, seven and four. Raised in an orphanage in Mindinao, they never had any opportunities to stretch themselves and find out what they could achieve. Their response to every task or challenge was, "We can't do that!"

I decided to teach these boys that they could do anything they wanted if they would persevere. So I took them to the big swimming pool at Rollins College and placed them in the care of swimming coach Harry Meisel and his son Kevin. I knew exactly what those four boys would say: "We can't swim!"

"Not yet," I replied, "but you will."

Harry and Kevin tossed the boys in the water and you know what? Those four boys were right. They couldn't swim. They sank. Harry and Kevin pulled them up, drained the water out of them, and showed them how to stay afloat. The boys sank again. Harry and Kevin pulled them up again. They sank again. It got pretty monotonous!

But at some point, amid all the glub-glub-glubbing and splashing and cries for help, something clicked. The littlest kid caught on first, and he started swimming like a guppie. Well, that shamed the other three. Soon all four boys grew gills and fins and started swimming like sharks! What's more, they loved it. Within a few years, three of those boys qualified for the Junior Olympics in Florida. The same boys who said "we can't swim!" became some of the top swimmers in the state! It all happened because they learned to persevere.

Faith

The character quality of faith involves believing and acting on promises and commands of God. This word "faith" is often misused. Some people think it means "blind belief in an idea for which there is no evidence," to which I say, "No way!" Faith is rational. It's rooted in reliable evidence and experience. Faith comes from seeing how God has worked in history and how He is working in our lives today.

Every choice man and choice woman needs to have the character quality of faith. People of faith make the best leaders, teachers, parents and role models. Why? Because they see themselves as accountable to a holy God for their words, decisions and behavior.

How do we encourage kids to become people of faith? We talk about our relationship with God at every opportunity. As God tells us in Deuteronomy 6:6-7, "These commandments that I give you today are to be upon your hearts. Impress them on your children. Talk about them when you sit at home and when you walk along the road, when you lie down and when you get up." Never miss an opportunity to encourage your child's faith.

And while you're talking to your kids about faith, put your faith into action. When you struggle with temptation or adversity, make godly choices that arise from your faith-relationship with God the Father. When you hit your thumb with a hammer, make sure your kids hear blessing and not cursing. Make sure you show Christlike compassion, courtesy and respect to your kids, your wife, your coworkers, your neighbors, the postman, and the kid who bags your groceries.

Model a lifestyle of prayer to your kids—and not just at mealtime and at bedtime. As a family, stop and ask God's protection for your family trip. Pray with your family about big decisions, such as a job change or a big move. When good things happen, pause with your kids to send up a heartfelt "Thank You, God!" Let your kids see that you are constantly connected to the Father through prayer.

Compassion

The character trait of compassion involves empathy for the hurting and needy, a desire to offer them encouragement, and an eagerness to help them carry their burdens. A compassionate person is willing to sacrifice his convenience in order to bless others. Compassion springs from an authentic love for people, not from a desire for recognition.

How do we encourage our kids to become choice young men and choice young women of compassion? First, preach compassion. Talk about the compassion of Christ and urge your kids to emulate His example.

Second, model compassion. Let your kids see you reaching out and helping your neighbors, the homeless, the hungry, the elderly, people in prisons, people in need. Bring your kids along as you visit the convalescent home, the Rescue Mission, or your church's outreach to the homeless. Roll up your sleeves, wade out into the sea of human need, and bring your kids along so that they can experience what compassion truly feels like.

Third, send your kids out on a mission of compassion. Encourage them to get involved with Habitat for Humanity's Summer Youth Blitz. Send them on a short-term mission with Adventures in Missions, Teen Missions International, or your church's youth mission to Mexico or the inner city. Once they start reaching out and helping people, they'll love it. Compassion will become a way of life—and an ingrained facet of their character.

Darrell Scott is a Christian dad who taught his kids to be compassionate and to reach out to the marginalized and less fortunate people around them. He taught his kids to be witnesses for Christ on their campus. His kids attended Columbine High School in Littleton, Colorado.

Once your kids start reaching out and helping people, they'll love it. Compassion will become a way of life— and an ingrained facet of their character.

On April 20, 1999, Darrell's daughter Rachel was sitting on the grass outside of the cafeteria, eating her lunch. Two boys in trenchcoats walked up to her. Just a day or two earlier, Rachel had talked to one of those boys about her relationship with Jesus Christ. She knew he was troubled and she had compassion for him, but the boy wanted nothing to do with Rachel's God.

On this day, that troubled youth took a gun from his trenchcoat, pointed it at Rachel, and shot her in the leg. Rachel got up to run, so the boy shot her again, this time through the chest. She fell to the grass, still alive.

The two boys then shot the boy next to Rachel eight or nine times, leaving him alive but paralyzed. They went into the crowded school cafeteria and tried to set off a pair of butane tanks rigged as bombs. By the grace of God, the bombs failed to detonate. Had the tanks exploded, up to 450 students would have died in a fiery inferno.

Frustrated that the bombs had failed, the boys went back outside. One crouched beside Rachael, lifted her head by the hair, and said, "Do you still believe in God?" She said, "Yes, I do." The boy said, "Then go be with Him." He fired the gun, shooting her through the temple.

Before those two young killers turned their guns on themselves and committed suicide, they murdered 12 students and 1 teacher. Other students were shot and wounded.

Several weeks after the Columbine killings, a student from the school visited Darrell Scott. The boy had been born with a physical deformity that affected his facial features and left him with a speech impediment. Because of his deformity, some of his classmates had cruelly nicknamed him "Alien."

"I want to tell you something about your daughter Rachel," the boy told this grieving father. "Rachel was always nice to me. Every day, she put her arm around me and said, 'How are you doing today?' And you know what, Mr. Scott? I saw her just an hour before they killed her. She hugged me and she said, 'Someday soon, we'll get some coffee and go to a movie, and we're going to have a good time.' And every night since she died, I cry and cry, because Rachel was the only person in school who was nice to me."

This world needs more choice people like Rachel Scott—people of compassion, people who will be the embracing arms of Jesus Christ to the hurting and friendless. We need to raise a generation of gentle, godly warriors and choice kids like Rachel Scott.

STANDING FIRM THROUGH TEMPTATION AND ADVERSITY

One of my favorite people in the Bible is Joseph, the choice man of God whose story is told in the book of Genesis. I wrote a book on the life of Joseph entitled *Unsinkable*.[1] He was the second youngest of the 12 sons of Jacob. He dreamed dreams and saw visions of the future—and his dreams and visions made his 10 older brothers jealous. They hated him so much that they pounced on him and sold him into slavery, and then told their father that he'd been killed by a wild animal.

Joseph was bought by Potiphar, an Egyptian army captain. Potiphar placed Joseph (who was a teenager at the time) in charge of everything he owned. Imagine being a high schooler and having your boss trust you with his checkbook, his credit cards, and even the keys to his new chariot!

One day, Potiphar's wife came to Joseph and tried to seduce him, but Joseph refused. "My master hasn't withheld anything in his house from me except you, his wife," he said. "How could I do such an evil thing to him and sin against God?" That's character talking. That's a choice man of God taking a stand for his integrity and faith in God.

Potiphar's wife was enraged by Joseph's refusal—so she set out to destroy him. When Potiphar returned, she accused Joseph of attempted rape. So Potiphar threw Joseph into prison. This choice man was rewarded with slander and injustice. That's the way the world often works: Sometimes we must pay a high price to do what's right—but a choice man is willing to pay that price, knowing that the price of sin is even greater.

Ultimately, Joseph's character and integrity won the attention of the Pharaoh, the ruler of Egypt. Pharaoh released Joseph from prison and made him the Number Two man over all of Egypt. Because of his faith and flawless character, Joseph won Pharoah's confidence.

Our kids will face temptation and adversity in life. We need to encourage them to build strong character and prepare themselves for the tough times ahead. Here are some ways we can inspire and motivate young people to build character to stand firm like Joseph.

Start Early

There's a lot of wisdom in the ancient proverb, "Train a child in the way he should go, and when he is old he will not turn from it" (Prov. 22:6). In other words, if you want to build choice men and choice women, you have to start with choice kids. If you want to raise your kids to follow and imitate Jesus, then you have to begin teaching faith and character from their earliest years.

Raise Your Children According to Their Unique Personality

When it comes to discipling kids, there is no such thing as "one size fits all." If you have 18 kids living in your house, then you need 18 parenting styles, one for each child in your family. And that means you need to take the time to get to know each child as a unique individual.

If you walked into the Williams house on Thanksgiving Day, you'd be confronted with a sea of faces. But when I look around our gigantic table, I see all of my individual children, each with his or her own dreams, talents, character traits, strengths, weaknesses, eccentricities and endearing qualities. You have to know each of your kids as an individual and then develop a parenting style to meet the needs of that individual human soul.

Some kids, for example, are awkward and insecure. Your job as a Christian dad is to give those kids your approval, validation, attention and affirmation. You need to give them opportunities to succeed and build their confidence.

You may have kids who are selfish, egotistical and insensitive to others. Your job as a Christian dad is to teach them how to be humble, patient and considerate of the feelings of others. You need to use a completely different set of parenting muscles with these kids than you use with the awkward and insecure kids.

Some of your kids may be tough, hard-headed and intensely committed to truth, but with little sense of grace and mercy. There are some good qualities there and some potential drawbacks. Your job is to find ways to teach those kids how to balance truth with grace, justice with mercy. Teach them to temper their toughness. Show them from the Scriptures that while Jesus never compromised the truth, He was always gracious and merciful to sinners and to people in need.

You may have kids who err on the side of being too merciful and emotional. They need to learn to show good rational judgment, to think as well as to feel. It's all right to feel sorry for the guy who claims he'll work for food—but show them by your own example that true compassion should be wise. You can say to your kids, "See what I did? Instead of giving him cash, which he might spend on drugs, I bought him a sandwich and I gave him a lift to the Rescue Mission. God wants us to be merciful—and wise!"

Instruct Your Kids Daily in the Truths of the Christian Faith

Attend church with your kids. Don't drop them at church and then drive away. You may say, "But my kids don't want to go to church!" Oh? Who gave them a vote? Rule Number One at the Williams house is: If you live under our roof, you go to church and Sunday School every week, no exceptions.

Even more important than the faith we practice on Sunday mornings is the faith we practice from Monday through Saturday. As Christian dads, we need to exemplify faith in the home every single day. That means we read the Scriptures and pray with our kids. We discuss issues of faith and values in the family daily, at mealtimes or whenever a situation comes up that would serve as an object lesson. God should not be an add-on in your family; He must be the foundation and focus of your family. And, Dad, it all begins with *you*.

Praise and Correct Your Kids on the Basis of Character

When a child breaks the rules, don't just punish the disobedience. Instead, point out how the disobedience harms his or her character. Say, "You want to build good character so that people will trust you and depend on you. The only way to build character is by making good decisions when you are tempted. The next time you're tempted, ask yourself, 'If I do this, will I build my character—or tear it down?'"

When a child does well, say, "I'm so proud of you! You're building good character! You're becoming more like Jesus. You're really growing in your integrity, courage, faith and sense of responsibility."

Let Your Kids Suffer the Consequences of Poor Choices

That's hard! Most Christian parents feel compassion for their kids and want to shield them, even from the natural repercussions of their sins and mistakes. But natural consequences are the best teachers. If you want to raise choice men and choice women of character, your kids need to understand that there is a price to pay for poor character and poor decisions. Resist the urge to rescue your kids.

Talk to Your Kids About Heroes

These are tough times for heroes. Again and again, we've seen so-called "heroes" demolished by their own character flaws. As columnist Leonard Pitts Jr. observed, "My middle son, Marlon, complained to me just the other day that his generation is coming of age in a world without heroes. . . . Our children have learned to wait for the other shoe to drop, for 'heroes' to be unmasked and values betrayed."

It's sad but true. All around us, we see sports heroes, political heroes, and religious leaders unmasked by scandal, their reputations shattered by sin. If you want to give your kids a pantheon of heroes to pattern their lives after, point them to Hebrews 11, a role call of choice men and choice women who exemplified faith, integrity, courage and every other admirable trait. These were people of such immense character that the writer of Hebrews concludes, "the world was not worthy of them" (v. 38).

Another suggestion: Tell your kids stories or watch movies together about heroes—choice men and choice women who have been tried and tested and have demonstrated great character. Then discuss that person's

---

If you want to raise choice men and choice women of character, your kids need to understand that there is a price to pay for poor character and poor decisions.

life with your kids and ask them what character qualities they spotted in the story.

Model a Lifestyle of Service to Others

Make sure your kids see you living out Christlike servanthood in your own life. Find ways to involve your kids in volunteerism and helping other people who are less fortunate than themselves. If you need ideas for local service projects for your kids, talk to your pastor or youth leader. Help your kids learn to think of others, not just themselves.

After the publication of my book *Coaching Your Kids to Be Leaders*, I received an e-mail from a reader, Tom Walsh.[2] He's starting early and teaching his kids to serve others. He wrote:

Thanks for writing this book! As a father of two boys, ages two and four (with a third child on the way), I found a lot of ideas in your book about how to raise emotionally and spiritually healthy kids. Your book inspired me to action.

Last Saturday, my wife was working and I was watching the boys. We started with a trip to their favorite bagel store. After that, we stopped by the local nursing home. I wanted to see if it would be possible for us to visit with some of the patients. I thought it might brighten their day, and it would be a good experience for my boys to learn the importance of helping others.

We went to the desk and the receptionist asked who we had come to visit. I said, "Anyone. We just want to visit someone who could use a little company." The receptionist was astonished! I guess this doesn't happen very often.

The nursing home staff was accommodating, and they gladly let us wander around and talk to people wherever we went. We eventually found our way to a lounge area where many of the residents had gathered for doughnuts and coffee.

My four-year-old, George, stepped right up to people, put out his hand, and (as I had coached him earlier) said, "Hi! My name is George! It's nice to meet you!" And he gave each person a hearty handshake. The people enjoyed his company, and it was a good experience for my boys. I never imagined a dad could be so proud of a four-year-old son!

I don't think you can ever start too early training kids to consider other people and serve them. At the same time, you are teaching them to sharpen their social skills, overcome shyness and build their confidence. That was an important first step in a leadership training process that I look forward to continuing throughout my kids' formative years. Thanks again for providing that spark of inspiration in your book!

Sincerely,
Tom Walsh

Now there's a father who gets it! I'm happy that my book inspired him—but his story inspired me even more. It's never too early to start teaching our kids to serve others.

Involve Your Kids in Sports and Scouting

There's nothing about running, throwing a ball, or hiking in the woods that automatically builds character. But sports and Scouting can have a profound influence on our kids if coaches, scoutmasters and parents exemplify good character traits.

Frosty Westering, former head football coach at Pacific Lutheran University, once said, "How a man plays the game shows something of his character. How he loses shows all of it." It's true. There's great character-building and character-exposing value for kids in both winning and losing when they are involved in sports. Kids learn to compete hard while respecting their opponents, coaches, officials and the rules of the game. When a young person learns good sportsmanship, he or she also learns good character.

And what about Scouting? While researching *Coaching Your Kids to Be Leaders*, I interviewed over 800 leaders in all walks of life. I was surprised to discover that roughly a third of respondents mentioned Scouting as one of the formative influences on their character and leadership ability.

Young Scouts make a commitment to be "trustworthy, loyal, helpful, friendly, courteous, kind, obedient, cheerful, thrifty, brave, clean and reverent." In short, Scouting is all about building good character! In recent years, the Boy Scouts have been under attack for being politically incorrect. I think these attacks on Scouting are a crime. I hope you will join me in promoting and defending Boy Scouts and Girl Scouts, two of the few movements in our society that still teach respect for God and country, moral virtue, good citizenship, and the principles of good character.

RAISING DESCENDENTS OF ASHER IN A POSTMODERN AGE

If you want to build choice kids of character, then you need to understand the world they live in and the worldly pressures that threaten to poison their minds and hearts. You need to be a student of your kids' world—their culture, their language, their values, their views.

Don't assume that they are growing up in the same teenage culture you did. Yes, they still listen to rock—but the rock they listen to is nothing like the Who, the 'Stones, or the Doors. Don't tune out their music just because it doesn't appeal to you. Be aware that some of the harshest-sounding music may come from a Christian band, while some of the most listenable tunes may contain messages of godless despair, drugs, sex, violence and suicide.

Your kids have grown up in a very different world from the one you and I were raised in. From their earliest years, they've been exposed to computers and other high-tech gadgetry. They can multitask much better than you and I ever could—e-mailing, instant messaging, web surfing, all while talking on the cell phone. They require constant noise and entertainment. They're Starbucks-addicted, hyperstimulated and impatient; as a result, they have short attention spans and are easily bored.

Your kids are part of a cyber-literate, Internet-savvy generation living in a global neighborhood. Odds are, your kids have friends they feel close to but have never met. These friends may live across the country or even on the other side of the world, yet your kids chat with them on a daily basis.

Young people today are steeped in the postmodern worldview. I won't take time here to explain all about postmodernism and where it came from, but here's what the world looks like through postmodern eyes.

Postmodern youth are more into feeling than thinking. They are more easily influenced by stories and experiences than by reason and logic. They don't believe in objective, absolute truth; they say, "You have your truth and I have mine." They often believe in a do-it-yourself spirituality. For them, it's okay to make up your own God and your own morality.

One of the highest values to postmoderns is tolerance, which they define as uncritical inclusion of differing views, lifestyles and cultures. As a result, the truth that Jesus declares in John 14:6 sounds narrow-minded and intolerant to many postmoderns: "I am the way and the truth and the life. No one comes to the Father except through me."

Even though most kids today don't believe in objective truth, they value trust. They place a premium on honesty and integrity, and they are watching to see if you're authentic. If they detect any hint that you have deceived or betrayed them, they will withdraw their trust.

Even if you raised them to be upright and moral, your kids have probably soaked up (from the media, the culture and their peers) a certain degree of belief that there is no absolute right or wrong. Surveys show that most kids (including church kids) think that pirating music and other copyrighted materials via "peer-to-peer" file-sharing websites is "cool." Tell them it's wrong to steal music from record companies and they'll say, "Rich record companies don't need my money!" That's not just a rationalization to them. They honestly feel no guilt, because in their worldview, if they want something, it's moral for them to have it.

Today's kids take a similar view of sexual morality: There are no objective standards. They see morality as something that each individual defines privately on the basis of feelings and preferences. Many kids make an arbitrary distinction between intercourse and so-called "outer-course"—sexual activity that does not involve sexual penetration. Some kids equate safety with morality: "Sex isn't immoral as long as it's *protected* sex." The average postmodern teen does not stop to think about the moral, psychological or spiritual consequences of sexual activity at an early age.

It's important that we understand how our kids view the world so that we can more effectively counter the corrosive postmodern thought patterns that infect their souls. Today more than ever before, young people need to build the truth of Romans 12:2 into their lives: "Do not conform any longer to the pattern of this world, but be transformed by the renewing of your mind."

If you want to raise choice kids who will take a stand for God in this godless postmodern world, learn to see the world through their eyes. Ask God to help you not to become frustrated or angry with their alien ways of thinking. Accept the fact that their thinking is nonlinear and that they are not persuaded by logical arguments. Our message to them should not be, "You're wrong. You need to change the way you think." Instead, our approach should be to find ways to communicate God's unchanging truth to them in ways that connect with their experience and their Internet-speed attention span.

If you want to raise choice kids who will take a stand for God in this godless postmodern world, learn to see the world through their eyes.

Talk to them about the messages in their music; instead of knocking their music for being "just a lot of noise and screaming," encourage them to get their noise and screaming from Christian bands whose songs have positive messages and lyrics. Encourage them to take regular breaks from the endless whirl of entertainment and stimulation. Limit TV, computer and Xbox time. Set an example by having both individual and family devotional time. Teach your kids what the Lord means when He says, "Be still, and know that I am God" (Ps. 46:10).

Be aware of your children's friends, because they will have an enormous influence on your kids. Teach your children what the Bible says about making friends and dealing with peer pressure: "He who walks with the wise grows wise, but a companion of fools suffers harm" (Prov. 13:20); "Do not be misled: 'Bad company corrupts good character'" (1 Cor. 15:33).

Equally important, be aware of what your kids are doing on the Internet. You should keep all computers out in an open family area, where kids can't hide their online activity. And don't think that online porn is the only danger your kid faces on the Internet.

Do your kids have web pages on MySpace.com? Do they visit chat rooms or do online instant messaging? If so, they are probably bombarded with obscene language, sex talk and flirting, R-rated and X-rated images, and an endless assault of immoral and antireligious ideas, opinions and jokes. The teenage web logs ("blogs") and chat rooms your kids visit are generally filled with sex talk, drug talk, hate talk and verbal abuse.

Take a good, hard look at your kids' lifestyle and ask yourself: What are my kids listening to on their iPods? Do they have an eating disorder, like anorexia or bulimia? Are my kids experimenting with drugs? Are they getting sucked into an unhealthy relationship at school or over the Internet? Do my kids have a video game addiction? Are they wasting too much time on the computer or on other forms of entertainment? Would their time be better spent in church, sports, music or Scouting activities?

Do you screen your kid's Internet use? I'm not talking about a filtering program. They haven't invented a kid-proof filter yet. I'm telling you that you need to spy on your kid. "What?" you say. "Invade my child's privacy?" I say: What privacy? Kids aren't entitled to complete privacy—not where their hearts, minds and souls are at stake. You bought the computer, you pay the broadband bills, you are responsible for what your kid does online. So you'd better know what's going on.

Above all, talk to your kids—and listen to them. Don't believe for a moment that you have no influence. Sure, they argue with you and dismiss everything that you say with a shrug. But after you leave the room and walk down the hall, they sift and ponder your advice. Sure, they may reject most of it—but some of what you say gets through. One day, you may even overhear them on the phone, talking to a friend, echoing the very message you gave them on drugs or sex or faith in Christ. Then you'll know that all the grief and aggravation was worth it. You're making a dent, you're having an influence—and you're watching character under construction.

THE TRUE HEART OF A FATHER

Your kids live in a tough world—a world that wants to ensnare and enslave them, make them feel inadequate, and shame them if they don't conform. The world will ridicule and curse your kids for being Christians and demonstrating a love for God.

As fathers in the Asher tradition, our job is to stand with our kids against the world—not to shield them, but to strengthen and empower them to face the temptations and fury of this world. Every time they're told, "You're nothing," we have to tell them ten times, a hundred times, "I love you! I'm proud of you!" Every time they fail, we need to say, "You can do it! I believe in you!" We need to affirm our kids and love them unconditionally.

Let me tell you a story about a father's unconditional love. I have known Julius Erving, the legendary Dr. J, since 1976 when I was general manager of the Philadelphia 76ers. In 1997, Julius joined the Orlando Magic organization as executive vice president, and we worked together in the front office for almost five years.

In early June of 2000, Julius called me with terrible news: his 19-year-old son, Cory, was missing. On May 28, Cory had driven to the store to buy bread for a Memorial Day cookout but had not returned. Julius was preparing to go public about Cory's disappearance and he asked me to serve as spokesman for the family. I was happy to help any way I could.

Life had not been easy for Cory. Afflicted with dyslexia and attention deficit disorder, he had struggled in school and had been through drug rehab several times as a teen. Some people, knowing about Cory's past problems, assumed he had run away from home. Julius didn't think so. He was sure something had happened to Cory. Before his disappearance, Cory had made constructive changes in his life. He had a job and was attending junior college. His relationship with his parents was good. Why would he run away? It didn't add up.

Julius posted a $25,000 reward and made a national appeal for help in finding Cory. On June 23, he appeared on CNN's *Larry King Live*. He affectionately described his son to Larry King, saying, "He has a lot of potential as a person. He's charming, he's clever, he's kind of kooky at times. . . . We want the public to help us bring back a person we love very much."

One caller to the Larry King show asked how Julius and his family were holding up through the crisis. "We're all doing well under the circumstances," he replied. "I've been holding dear to my heart the Scriptures, in particular Luke 15:11, the parable of the prodigal son. That passage says that in the end, we will all celebrate because our son was lost and now is found. When our son comes home, we'll have a feast and a celebration."

At the end of the segment, Larry King gave Julius a few moments for a final word. Julius looked into the camera and said, "Cory, if you're watching this show, come home. I don't care where you are or what you've done, we love you unconditionally. We miss you. We want you back and we need you back. We love you, son. Please call us and come home."

Two weeks passed with no word from Cory. On Thursday, July 6, Seminole County sheriff's deputies made a discovery while combing a retention pond. They found Cory's black Volkswagen Passat in eight feet of water. Cory was inside. His death was an accident.

After Cory was found, Julius asked me to put out a brief statement to the media: "I would like to thank Sheriff Eslinger and his staff for returning our son to us." Julius Erving's lost son came home, and just as he had promised on Larry King's show, he held a feast for family and friends to celebrate the return of a much-loved son.

The apostle Paul described the heart of a father like Julius Erving when he wrote, "For you know that we dealt with each of you as a father deals with his own children, encouraging, comforting and urging you to live lives worthy of God, who calls you into his kingdom and glory" (1 Thess. 2:11-12). That's the kind of loving, compassionate, affirming father Asher was, and the kind of father you and I should aspire to be.

As we let our kids know they are loved, affirmed and valued, we armor them against the assaults and pressures of this world. We strengthen them to stand firm against the temptation and adversity of this world. Through our unconditional love and affirmation, we enable our kids to truly become choice kids and spiritual descendents of Asher.

Notes

1. Pat Williams with David Wimbish, *Unsinkable: Getting Out of Life's Pits and Staying Out* (Grand Rapids, MI: Fleming Revell Publishers, 2002).
2. Pat Williams, *Coaching Your Kids to Be Leaders: The Keys to Unlocking Their Potential* (New York: Warner Faith, 2005).

DIMENSION 3:
BOLDNESS

IMAGINE A WARRIOR . . .

Five years had passed since Ishvah had given his prized bow and arrows to his friend Arad. Now Ishvah's world had turned dark. Arad lay dead at Ishvah's feet.

Asher stood at Ishvah's side, looking down at Arad's twisted, bloody remains. Two of Ishvah's brothers, Imnah and Ishvi, stood nearby, looking around the ransacked house of Elkanah the Metalsmith. By the door were the bodies of Elkanah and his wife Baara, their arms intertwined in death. Across the room were the bodies of a servant girl and Arad's younger sister, Naarah.

All around the room furniture was smashed into kindling. Cloth bags were spilled and strewn around. Elkanah's metalworking tools were scattered across the floor, along with ingots of iron and sheets of hammered brass. But there was no gold or silver in the house; it had all been stolen. An entire family had been butchered for a few pounds of shiny metal.

"They never had a chance," said Imnah, The Chieftain. His dark eyes smoldered with rage.

"The Midianites will pay," said Ishvi, whom Asher called The Philosopher.

"Where's the bow?" asked Ishvah, The Warrior, kneeling beside his dead friend.

Asher frowned. "Where is what?"

"The longbow you made for me," Ishvah said. "I gave it to Arad five years ago. He always kept it by the door. The Midianites must have taken it."

"We should bury them," said Ishvah's younger brother, Ishvi.

"You bury them!" Ishvah snapped angrily. "I'm going to hunt down the Midianites who did this!"

"We can't leave Elkanah and his family like this," Asher said. "We'll take the bodies to the tomb."

In life, Elkanah was a man of substance. He had a tomb carved out of a hillside not far from his house. It didn't take Asher and his sons long to move the five bodies into the cool darkness of the tomb. After saying a prayer, Asher and his sons went in search of the killers.

It wasn't hard to follow the tracks of the Midianites. They trampled the ground like a herd of oxen. The trail led east, toward the Gzelah Pass. From the tracks, Asher determined that there were 18 to 20 raiders—far too many to attack in the open. But Gzelah Pass was a narrow, rock-walled defile, perfectly suited for an ambush.

"Imnah," Asher said as they walked, addressing his first-born son, "you will follow the raiders through the western gate of the pass. Don't let them know you're behind them until you hear my shout."

Imnah nodded.

"Ishvah and Ishvi, we'll scale the talus slope to the south of the pass. You'll position yourselves on the cliff top to ambush them from above. I'll make for the east end of the defile to cut off their escape."

Ishvah and Ishvi nodded.

The sun was directly overhead when Asher and his sons sprung their trap. The Midianites were startled by a shout that came from in front of them. A rain of arrows fell on them from above, out of the blinding sun. The Midianites panicked and broke ranks. Some ran back the way they came, directly into Imnah's arrows. Others tried to press forward, where they fell screaming, pierced through the throat and chest by Asher's arrows.

The slaughter did not last long. When the last Midianite screams and curses echoed away, Elkanah and his family were avenged. Asher and his sons stripped the pouches of gold and silver from the bodies. Ishvah found his old longbow on the ground next to one of the fallen Midianites.

Leaving the dead for the vultures, Asher and his three warrior-sons returned to the cave where the family of Elkanah the Metalsmith lay in the cool shadows. Asher placed the gold and silver beside the body of Elkanah. Ishvah placed the longbow on Arad's chest and folded his hands over it.

Asher and his sons piled many stones over the mouth of the tomb, sealing it well. Only when they had finished did Ishvah fall to his knees and weep uncontrollably over the loss of his friend. His fellow warriors—his father and his brothers—knelt beside him and mingled their tears with his.

Be a Warrior for God

I raised my kids to be warriors. Two of them, Peter and David, have served in the United States Marine Corps. David, who is still on active duty, is a veteran of Operation Iraqi Freedom. He saw the death and devastation of war firsthand.

On one occasion, David was on a mission with a motor convoy that nearly ended in disaster. The young lieutenant in charge decided to take a shortcut. The convoy, consisting of 20 vehicles and 40 Marines, got lost. They soon found themselves boxed into a very dangerous position, with a deadend ahead, a canal on the right, a raised berm on the left, and the road so narrow they couldn't back out.

"Our lieutenant started to freak out," David recalled. "There were Iraqi townspeople all around, watching this in amazement."

The Marines knew that word was already being passed to the Iraqi forces. If David and his buddies didn't find a way out—and fast—they would become tomorrow's headlines.

"At that point," David recalled, "the first sergeant took over. He was calm and organized—a quick thinker. He told a bunch of guys, 'Dig out the berm so we can get the vehicles moving, and then we'll turn around.' The sarge had a plan and he got us all on the same page. Somehow we made it out before the Iraqi troops found us."

David made it home from that war. A lot of his fellow soldiers didn't. Let me tell you about a few of the warriors of that war, selected at random from the roll call of those who paid the ultimate price for freedom.

Marine Lance Corporal José Gutierrez of Los Angeles died at age 22. He was one of the first U.S. soldiers killed in Operation Iraqi Freedom, and he wasn't even an American citizen. Born in Guatemala, orphaned as

Be a Warrior for God

I raised my kids to be warriors. Two of them, Peter and David, have served in the United States Marine Corps. David, who is still on active duty, is a veteran of Operation Iraqi Freedom. He saw the death and devastation of war firsthand.

On one occasion, David was on a mission with a motor convoy that nearly ended in disaster. The young lieutenant in charge decided to take a shortcut. The convoy, consisting of 20 vehicles and 40 Marines, got lost. They soon found themselves boxed into a very dangerous position, with a deadend ahead, a canal on the right, a raised berm on the left, and the road so narrow they couldn't back out.

"Our lieutenant started to freak out," David recalled. "There were Iraqi townspeople all around, watching this in amazement."

The Marines knew that word was already being passed to the Iraqi forces. If David and his buddies didn't find a way out—and fast—they would become tomorrow's headlines.

"At that point," David recalled, "the first sergeant took over. He was calm and organized—a quick thinker. He told a bunch of guys, 'Dig out the berm so we can get the vehicles moving, and then we'll turn around.' The sarge had a plan and he got us all on the same page. Somehow we made it out before the Iraqi troops found us."

David made it home from that war. A lot of his fellow soldiers didn't. Let me tell you about a few of the warriors of that war, selected at random from the roll call of those who paid the ultimate price for freedom.

Marine Lance Corporal José Gutierrez of Los Angeles died at age 22. He was one of the first U.S. soldiers killed in Operation Iraqi Freedom, and he wasn't even an American citizen. Born in Guatemala, orphaned as a young boy, Gutierrez was 14 when he reached California as an undocumented alien, hiding in a railway boxcar. He grew up in Los Angeles, learned English, lived in group homes, and always looked out for the younger kids who were growing up without families. He joined the Marines after the September 11 terrorist attacks because, as he put it, "I came here with nothing. This country gave me everything." He was killed on March 21, 2003, in fighting near the port city of Umm Qasr.

Army Chief Warrant Officer Brian K. Van Dusen was a 39-year-old warrior of the 571st Medical Company (Air Ambulance). On May 9, 2003, he flew his UH-60 Black Hawk helicopter to a site near Samarrah. His mission: to evacuate an 11-year-old child who had stepped on an Iraqi landmine. While approaching the landing site near the Tigris River, the helicopter snagged a pulley cable and flipped over into the water. Van Dusen and two crewmates were killed. The child was airlifted by another helicopter and survived. Brian Van Dusen was a warrior whose job was saving lives. He left behind a wife and three small children.

Army Sergeant Michael T. Crockett was a bold warrior, a thoughtful husband, and a doting father who enjoyed surprising his wife with unexpected gifts. The 27-year-old soldier from Soperton, Georgia, was on patrol in Baghdad on July 14, 2003, when his truck was hit by Iraqi rocket-propelled grenades. He was killed in the attack and 10 of his fellow warriors were wounded. The next day, a dozen red roses arrived at the home of Sergeant Crockett's wife, Tracey; he had ordered them shortly before he was killed. Only a few hours after the roses were delivered, soldiers arrived at her door with the news that she was a widow.

Army Sergeant Michael D. Acklin II of Louisville, Kentucky, was 25 when he died in a crash of two Black Hawk helicopters near Mosul on November 15, 2003. He was one of 17 soldiers killed in the accident. Sergeant Acklin dreamed of going to Bible college and entering the ministry after serving his time in the Army. His father, Michael D. Acklin, Sr., said, "He fought and died trusting in Jesus. That's what motivated his life." At his funeral, Sergeant Acklin's pastor said the young warrior had "fought the good fight of a soldier and fought the good fight of faith."

Navy Equipment Operator Christopher M. Dickerson of Eastman, Georgia, was killed on April 30, 2004, when his convoy vehicle was destroyed by an improvised explosive device in Anbar Province. Dickerson was a man known for his gift for making people laugh. At his memorial service, a story was told of the time Dickerson portrayed the apostle John in a church play. During the Last Supper scene, he ate every piece of fruit from the fruit bowl. Throughout the scene, the rest of the cast members struggled to keep a straight face and say their lines. Though a prankster, Dickerson was serious about the Christian faith. He often spoke with amazement about all that Jesus did in His 33 years on Earth. Like his Lord, this gentle warrior was only 33 when he died.

The list could go on for hundreds of pages. The point I'm making is a simple one. The people of our armed forces are good people serving in a noble profession. They are warriors.

THE WARRIOR AND WAR

Let's get this said right away: War is evil and stupid. One of the greatest warriors in history put it this way: "I hate war as only a soldier who has lived it can—as one who has seen its brutality, its futility, its stupidity." These words are from General Dwight Eisenhower, Supreme Commander of the Allied forces in Europe in World War II.

From a biblical perspective, we know that war is the result of human sin, hate and selfishness. If you read the Bible from Genesis to Revelation, you read of war after war after war. You will never find war condemned in the Bible, nor will you find it glorified. The Bible simply acknowledges that war is a fact of life in this fallen world in which we live.

Jesus never said that military service was sinful. In fact, He respected military service and military men. He knew that warriors are a force for

Jesus never said that military service was sinful. In fact, He respected military service and military men. He knew that warriors are a force for good in the world.

good in the world. Early in His ministry, Jesus was in his adopted hometown of Capernaum when a Roman warrior, a centurion, came to him for help. "Lord," the Roman said, "my servant lies at home paralyzed and in terrible suffering."

"I will go and heal him," Jesus said.

"Lord," the Roman warrior replied, "I do not deserve to have you come under my roof. But just say the word, and my servant will be healed. For I myself am a man under authority, with soldiers under me. I tell this one, 'Go,' and he goes; and that one, 'Come,' and he comes."

Jesus was astounded to hear such words—and from a Roman! "I tell you the truth," He said, "I have not found anyone in Israel with such great faith" (see Matt. 8:5-10).

Jesus respected the warrior profession, because it is an honorable profession. Warriors prepare for war, but their goal is peace. "To be prepared for war," George Washington said, "is one of the most effectual means of preserving peace." Though war is an evil thing, warriors are a force for good in the world.

Warriors backed the Declaration of Independence with bullets and blood. They planted their boots in the bloody crossroads of history and they turned 13 oppressed colonies into a free nation.

Warriors fought the Civil War and enforced the Emancipation Proclamation of Abraham Lincoln. With their own blood, they purchased the freedom of four million slaves.

During World War II, warriors landed at Salerno, Anzio and Normandy. They fought their way across Europe and rolled back Nazi aggression. They opened the concentration camps and ended the Holocaust.

Warriors answered the attack on Pearl Harbor with daring raids over Tokyo. They endured the Bataan death march and landed at Guadalcanal, Iwo Jima and Okinawa. They waded ashore in the Philippines, and they dropped the bombs that stunned the world and brought the war to a halt.

Warriors fought unpopular actions in Korea and Vietnam. They received no thanks, no homecoming parades. But these warriors didn't complain. They just did their jobs and then quietly returned to their lives.

Warriors liberated Kuwait from the occupation of Sadaam Hussein. Warriors went into Afghanistan and liberated oppressed people from religious extremists and terrorists. Warriors liberated Iraq, pulled Saddam Hussein out of his spider hole, built new schools and water treatment facilities, and made it possible for the Iraqi people to hold a free election for the first time in their history.

The apostle Paul once wrote that the one who wields the sword on behalf of the government is "God's servant, an agent of wrath to bring punishment on the wrongdoer" (Rom. 13:4). Warriors serve God by punishing evil and keeping society secure and at peace.

THE LORD IS A WARRIOR!

In Exodus 14, we read that God's servant Moses led the nation of Israel out of captivity in Egypt. God miraculously parted the Red Sea so that the people of Israel could cross. Then, after the Israelites had reached the other side, God closed the waters once more. The Egyptians who pursued them perished and Israel was saved. Exodus 15 records the song of deliverance that Moses taught Israel as a prayer to the Lord:

> The LORD is my strength and my song;
> he has become my salvation.
> He is my God, and I will praise him,
> my father's God, and I will exalt him.
> The LORD is a warrior;
> the LORD is his name (vv. 2-3).

Notice those words: The Lord is a warrior! God is a Warrior-King who makes war against evil and defends the righteous—and you and I are made in His image and likeness! We are warriors, too. He is our example, our role model, the One who draws up the plan of battle and leads us into the fray. The Lord is our King and the Lord is a warrior.

As our Warrior-King, He makes us mighty in battle. He summons forth our courage and our will to fight. He prepares us for war. We see this principle in the life of Joshua.

After the death of Moses, the Lord spoke to Joshua and appointed him to be Moses' successor. Joshua's assignment: to lead Israel across the Jordan River and into the land of promise. The Lord told Joshua that there would be battles ahead and that Joshua would have to lead the nation through a time of war. But the Lord also prepared Joshua and promised to be with him in every battle. "As I was with Moses," God said, "so I will be with you; I will never leave you nor forsake you" (Josh. 1:5). Then God told Joshua the secret of success in battle: God's own Word.

> Do not let this Book of the Law depart from your mouth; medi-
> tate on it day and night, so that you may be careful to do every-
> thing written in it. Then you will be prosperous and successful.
> Have I not commanded you? Be strong and courageous. Do not
> be terrified; do not be discouraged, for the LORD your God will
> be with you wherever you go (vv. 8-9).

After Joshua died, Israel sank into complacency and disobedience. As a result, the nation came under the oppression of foreign enemies. The Midianites and Amalekites invaded, ruining the crops and stealing the livestock. During this time of oppression, an angel of the Lord appeared to a man named Gideon and said, "The LORD is with you, mighty warrior."

Hearing this, Gideon was sure the angel had the wrong guy! He thought, *I'm not a warrior—I'm a farmer!* But God knew Gideon better than Gideon knew himself. Somewhere inside this farm boy beat the heart of a warrior. Like you and me, Gideon was a warrior within! The angel said, "Go in the strength you have and save Israel out of Midian's hand."

Gideon protested, "But Lord, how can I save Israel? My clan is the weakest in Manasseh, and I am the least in my family."

God answered, "I will be with you, and you will strike down all the Midianites together" (see Judg. 6:12-16). And God made Gideon victorious in battle. Gideon's God is a warrior, and He transformed Gideon into a mighty warrior as well.

King David was also a warrior, made in the image of his Lord, the Warrior-King Jehovah. "Who is this King of glory?" David wrote in the Psalms. "The LORD strong and mighty, the LORD mighty in battle" (Ps. 24:8). And in the book of 2 Samuel, King David sang of how God, his Warrior-King, had trained him for war:

It is God who arms me with strength
and makes my way perfect . . .
He trains my hands for battle;
my arms can bend a bow of bronze (vv. 33,35).

Jesus, too, is a warrior. We see His warriorhood most clearly, of course, in Revelation 19. In that prophecy of the Last Days, heaven opens and Jesus appears astride a white warhorse, dressed in a robe spattered with blood. "With justice He judges and makes war," the Scriptures say. "He treads the winepress of the fury of the wrath of God Almighty" (vv. 11,15).

That is a future image of Christ Triumphant, when He returns to roll up the scroll of history and judge the world. But don't the four gospels portray Him as the Good Shepherd, the Lamb of God, the compassionate Friend of Sinners? Yes—but they also portray Him as a Warrior. As the Good Shepherd, He is a warrior against the enemies of His flock. As the sacrificial Lamb of God, He was nailed to the cross so that He could do battle against sin and death. As a Friend to Sinners, He is the warrior who has won the victory over Satan, the enemy and accuser of our souls.

Throughout the gospels, we see Jesus engaged in all-out warfare against the corrupt religious leaders of His day. He confronted them, argued with them, called them hypocrites to their faces, exposed their lies and traps, and made fools of them. It was a war of wits—and Jesus

A warrior who goes to war to liberate the oppressed and defend the innocent is a *peacemaker* in the truest sense of the word.

always wielded superior firepower! He never wielded a sword, but His battle against the religious corruption was a life-and-death struggle. From the beginning of His ministry, His enemies plotted to kill Him. Although He didn't look like a warrior on the outside, He was every bit a warrior within!

But didn't Jesus say, "Blessed are the peacemakers, for they will be called sons of God" (Matt. 5:9)? Yes, He did. But all true warriors love peace! They maintain the peace by being prepared for war. A warrior who goes to war to liberate the oppressed and defend the innocent is a *peacemaker* in the truest sense of the word.

Jesus told Pontius Pilate, "My kingdom is not of this world. If it were, my servants would fight" (John 18:36). Jesus was not fighting to control a piece of earthly real estate. His kingdom is not of this world. His battle is not a battle of swords and shields. His kingdom is a spiritual kingdom. The warfare He wages is *spiritual warfare*.

Just as the kingdom of Jesus is not of this world, the peace He brings is not a peace the world understands. "Peace I leave with you; my peace I give you," He said. "I do not give to you as the world gives. Do not let your hearts be troubled and do not be afraid" (John 14:27). The peace that Jesus gives us is not the absence of war. His peace is peace with God. He brings us this peace by defeating the enemy of our souls: "The reason the Son of God appeared was to destroy the devil's work" (1 John 3:8).

Throughout the four gospels, we see that the gentleness and peacefulness of Jesus were facets of His warriorhood. Although He was always gentle and kind to the poor and oppressed, Jesus continually battled the powerful and the oppressors.

Jesus the Warrior-King did not come to kill. He came to die. Jesus always knew what hill He would die on. The name of that hill was Calvary. His battlefield was a rugged wooden cross. And after the Warrior-King fought and bled and died upon that cross, something amazing happened: The power of death itself was destroyed! The apostle Paul put it this way:

> Then the end will come, when he hands over the kingdom to
> God the Father after he has destroyed all dominion, authority

and power. For he must reign until he has put all his enemies under his feet. The last enemy to be destroyed is death (1 Cor. 15:24-26).

Jesus is a warrior. And we, His followers, are warriors, too. Like our Warrior-King, we are gentle toward those in need. And like Him, we confront evil and injustice. Jesus calls us to lay hold of His kingdom, the kingdom of heaven, the kingdom that is not of this world. "From the days of John the Baptist until now," He said, "the kingdom of heaven has been forcefully advancing, and forceful men lay hold of it" (Matt. 11:12).

Forceful men like Asher lay hold of it. Warriors like you and me lay hold of it. We are the fierce and forceful men who must lay hold of the Kingdom and advance the cause of King Jesus. Deep within our hearts and souls, we know that we are warriors.

THE SEVEN VIRTUES OF A WARRIOR

In 1 Chronicles 7:40, we read that the descendants of Asher were "heads of families, choice men, *brave warriors* and outstanding leaders. The number of men *ready for battle*, as listed in their genealogy, was 26,000" (emphasis added). Before we can begin to raise generations of brave warriors, we must ask ourselves: *What does it truly mean to be a warrior?*

A warrior is a man who is trained, equipped and prepared for battle. He's a man of courage and moral conviction, willing to risk everything for a cause greater than himself. He's a man who is ready to yield up his one and only irreplaceable life for his king and commander.

The role of the warrior is a long and honorable tradition. Between the eleventh and fourteenth centuries A.D., the Japanese warrior class (the Samurai) developed a strict but unwritten code of conduct called *bushido*, the Way of the Warrior. This moral code was handed down warrior to warrior, from master to pupil, generation to generation. It was not written in books but, as historian Inazo Nitobe noted, "on the fleshly tables of the heart." There are seven *bushido* virtues that are revered by all true warriors:

義　(*Gi*) Moral rectitude or righteousness

勇　(*Yu*) Courage

仁　(*Jin*) Benevolence, the desire to do good

礼　(*Rei*) Humble respect for others

誠　(*Makoto*) Honesty

名誉　(*Meiyo*) Honor, esteem for oneself

忠義　(*Chuugi*) Loyalty and fidelity

In the early 1700s, the warrior wisdom of *bushido* was collected into two books. One, *Hagakure* by Yamamoto Tsunetomo, taught that *bushido* should be viewed not so much as a way of living but as a way of dying. The Samurai warrior must consider himself dead already so that he is willing to yield up his life at any moment in service to his lord. The other book, *Budoshoshinshu: The Code of the Warrior* by Daidoji Yuzan, also talked of the warrior's duty to lay down his life for his lord. Here is a typical passage from *Budoshoshinshu*:

> A warrior is a man who is determined to serve with the primary understanding that he will give up his one important life for his lord . . . He will not move one foot in retreat and will die a resplendent death, or else will stand in front of his lord or general, stopping the arrows loosed by the enemy with his own body.

A warrior, then, is a man who lives to die. Once a man is reconciled to death, he has every bit of courage it takes to be a warrior. He can take any risk, because he has nothing to lose. He can withstand any opposition, any criticism, any attack, because there is nothing anyone can do to him. He can persevere against any opponent, any opposition and any obstacle, because once he is resigned to death, surrender is unthinkable.

That is the model for the warrior within each of us. We live to die, we accept any risk God requires of us, and we are relentless against opposition and attack. The warrior within us is 1,000 percent committed and doesn't know the meaning of "surrender."

What is the cause that *you* are committed to, body and soul? What is the cause for which *you* are prepared to die?

Dr. Martin Luther King, Jr., was a warrior for peace and justice. He was prepared to die for his cause. He lived in a modest house in a poor neighborhood in Montgomery, Alabama, and he drove a secondhand Nash Rambler. As a young pastor, he led the Montgomery bus boycott in 1955 after a black woman, Rosa Parks, refused to give up her seat to a white man. During the 381 days of the boycott, Dr. King's life was threatened, he was arrested, and he was vilified in the news media.

One night in January 1956, Dr. King went to a meeting at a church near his home. During the meeting, someone burst in and shouted, "Dr. King! Somebody fire-bombed your house!" Dr. King's heart nearly failed him. His wife and baby were in the house! He drove home and arrived to see smoke rising from the front of his house. A crowd stood in the front yard. The bomb had exploded on the porch, shattering the windows and blackening the walls.

To his relief, Dr. King found his wife and baby safe inside the home. Outside his home, the crowd seethed with rage. People had guns and broken bottles in their hands and were engaged in a tense confrontation with police. Violence seemed inevitable.

Dr. King put his hands up to silence the crowd. "My wife and baby are all right," he said. "We have the weapon of nonviolence, the breastplate of righteousness, the armor of truth. We will not solve our problems with violence, because that would only harm our cause. Remember what the Bible tells us: 'Do not be overcome by evil, but overcome evil with good.'"

A few suspenseful seconds passed—and then someone in the crowd said, "God bless you, Dr. King!" The crowd dispersed.

The nonviolent bus boycott continued. In the end, Dr. King's peaceful war ended the illegal racial segregation on public buses. He was a warrior who committed himself to a dream that "one day this nation will rise up and live out the true meaning of its creed: 'We hold these truths to be self-evident: that all men are created equal.'"

Dr. King waged a nonviolent war—yet he paid a price in blood. On April 3, 1968, he stood before a crowd in Tennessee. "Like anybody," he said, "I would like to live a long life. Longevity has its place, but I'm not concerned about that now. I just want to do God's will. And He's allowed me to go up to the mountain. And I've looked over, and I've seen the Promised Land. I may not get there with you. But I want you to know tonight, that we, as a people, will get to the Promised Land. . . . Mine eyes have seen the glory of the coming of the Lord."

The next evening, at one minute past six o'clock, Dr. King stood on the balcony of his second-floor room at the Lorraine Motel in Memphis. As he stood alone on the balcony, a rifle shot sounded, echoing in the streets. Dr. King fell, shot in the jaw. He was pronounced dead at St. Joseph's Hospital one hour and four minutes later.

One of his closest friends was Dr. Andrew Young. A fellow pastor and civil rights activist, Dr. Young shared Dr. King's belief in nonviolent resistance. "I once heard Dr. King give a sermon on leadership, unity, and suffering," Dr. Young told me in a phone conversation. "He was willing to suffer for what he believed in. He'd laugh and joke with us about who would be the first one killed. He had a comic routine where he'd be preaching your funeral. He'd act it all out and made it very funny. That was his way of dealing with the inevitability of his death."

Everyone is afraid to die—even warriors. But the courage of a warrior gives him the strength to do the thing he fears. It gives him the will to wade into the battle, risking loss, pain and death for the sake of that which is greater than himself. The warrior within would rather die a resplendent death in battle than move one foot in retreat.

Spiritual Warfare

Some warriors wield swords. Some are armed with guns and bayonets. Some ride in tanks or Humvees, battleships or supersonic aircraft. And some are engaged in a very different kind of war. They wage *spiritual warfare*.

Spiritual warfare is every bit as real as battlefield warfare. In some ways, it is even *more* real, because the stakes involved in spiritual warfare

The warrior within would rather die a resplendent death in battle than move one foot in retreat.

are eternal. This war has been going on since before the human race existed. It is being fought all around us and within us, even as you read these words. It's a war in which each of us must choose sides. In *Waking the Dead*, John Eldredge puts it this way:

> We are at war. . . . How I've missed this for so long is a mystery to me. Maybe I've overlooked it; maybe I've chosen not to see. . . . The world in which we live is a combat zone, a violent clash of kingdoms, a bitter struggle unto the death. I'm sorry if I'm the one to break this news to you: you were born into a world at war, and you will live all your days in the midst of a great battle, involving all the forces of heaven and hell.[1]

C. S. Lewis, in *Mere Christianity*, makes a similar observation:

> One of the things that surprised me when I first read the New Testament seriously was that it talked so much about a Dark Power in the universe—a mighty evil spirit who was held to be the Power behind death, and disease, and sin. . . . Enemy-occupied territory—that is what this world is. Christianity is the story of how the rightful king has landed, you might say landed in disguise, and is calling us all to take part in a great campaign of sabotage.[2]

The apostle Paul has vividly described for us the nature of the battle we face. "For our struggle is not against flesh and blood," he wrote, "but against the rulers, against the authorities, against the powers of this dark world and against the spiritual forces of evil in the heavenly realms" (Eph. 6:12). Eldredge, Lewis and Paul agree: You and I are truly behind enemy lines, engaged in a life-or-death struggle. We are warriors on a mission of sabotage against spiritual forces of evil. These forces are invisible but deadly.

Don't make the mistake of thinking that you are living in peacetime. Don't think you are a noncombatant, a civilian. You're either a warrior or you're a casualty. There's no middle ground. So you'd better take up your weapon and fight.

As the apostle Paul told his spiritual son Timothy, "Endure hardship with us like a good soldier of Christ Jesus. No one serving as a soldier gets involved in civilian affairs—he wants to please his commanding officer" (2 Tim. 2:3-4). There will be hardship and suffering in this war. The enemy is gunning for you. Since you're already a target, you'd better make yourself a *hardened* target. You'd better put on some spiritual body armor.

SPIRITUAL BODY ARMOR

In Ephesians 6, the apostle Paul talks about the spiritual armor that every warrior needs when he goes into battle. He writes:

> Finally, be strong in the Lord and in his mighty power. Put on the full armor of God so that you can take your stand against the devil's schemes. For our struggle is not against flesh and blood, but against the rulers, against the authorities, against the powers of this dark world and against the spiritual forces of evil in the heavenly realms. Therefore put on the full armor of God, so that when the day of evil comes, you may be able to stand your ground, and after you have done everything, to stand. Stand firm then, with the belt of truth buckled around your waist, with the breastplate of righteousness in place, and with your feet fitted with the readiness that comes from the gospel of peace. In addition to all this, take up the shield of faith, with which you can extinguish all the flaming arrows of the evil one. Take the helmet of salvation and the sword of the Spirit, which is the word of God. And pray in the Spirit on all occasions with all kinds of prayers and requests (vv. 10-18).

Let's take a closer look at each of those pieces of spiritual body armor.

The Belt of Truth

First, Paul talks about *the belt of truth*. Warriors of Paul's day wore a belt with a scabbard for holding their swords. Warriors in today's infantry wear ammo belts for storing ammunition for their M16 rifles. Either way you look at it, the belt of truth symbolizes a warrior's integrity and honesty. Your truthfulness and the wholeness of your character are crucial factors in armoring your soul against the attack of the enemy.

If you live as a hypocrite, with habits of sin hidden in the dark corners of your life, then you are heading for spiritual defeat. If you compromise your truthfulness and integrity, then you might as well hand your ammo belt and weapon over to the enemy and surrender. He's got you where he wants you.

Never surrender your integrity. Never compromise the truth. Be a warrior through and through. Put on the belt of truth.

The Breastplate of Righteousness

Next, Paul says to wear *the breastplate of righteousness*. The Roman warriors of Paul's time wore a cuirass, consisting of a breastplate attached to a backplate, so that the body was protected from throat to waist by hard metal armor. Today's warriors in dangerous places like Iraq and Afghanistan wear a similar protective device called an OTV, or outer tactical vest.

On June 2, 2005, Army Private Stephen Tschiderer was standing beside his Humvee while on a routine patrol in western Baghdad. Seventy-five yards away, an enemy sniper was hidden in a van. The sniper aimed a Russian Dragunov 7.62 x 54 carbine through a hole in the side of the van and fired—and Private Tschiderer was hit in the chest. He was knocked backwards and down to the ground. He rolled once, jumped to his feet with his weapon raised, and positioned himself behind the Humvee. Though Private Tschiderer knew that he'd been hit, he didn't know how bad his wound was. His only thought was to locate the enemy and take him out. The shot had come from "twelve o'clock," directly in front of him. A van on the far side of the intersection was the only place the shot could have come from.

Tschiderer and the rest of his patrol team fired, causing two terrorists to run out of the van and flee on foot. The patrol team followed a trail of blood until they found the sniper lying wounded on the ground. Tschiderer himself handcuffed the man who had shot him, then took out a first aid kit and treated the sniper's wounds.

Later, Private Tschiderer checked his throbbing upper chest to see how badly he'd been shot. He found a purple bruise about the size of a grapefruit—located directly over his heart. The bullet that had been intended to kill him had been stopped by the hard ceramic SAPI (small arms protective insert) plate of his OTV. Without that "breastplate," he would have been killed.

The breastplate protects a warrior's heart. The breastplate of righteousness protects your confidence and courage. It defends you against the accusations and temptations of the enemy. When we commit our lives to Jesus Christ, He covers us with His righteousness and cancels out our sin. Then, through the power of the Holy Spirit, we are able to live righteous lives. Sure, we'll sin—and when we do, the enemy will say, "Look at you! You've failed!" At such times, we need the breastplate of the righteousness of Jesus. We need to say, "My Lord and Commander has promised to cover me with His righteousness and put me back into service for Him!"

Don't listen to the accuser. Don't fear him. His destruction is coming. The book of Revelation describes the ultimate end of the enemy of our souls:

> The accuser of our brothers,
> who accuses them before our God day and night,
> has been hurled down (Rev. 12:10).

So protect your warrior's heart. Wear the breastplate of righteousness. With your spiritual body armor in place, the enemy can shoot you, he can even knock you down—but you always can get back on your feet and go after your enemy! Why? Because, with the breastplate of righteousness in place, your warrior's heart is *bulletproof.*

With your spiritual body armor in place, the enemy can shoot you or even knock you down—but you always can get back on your feet and go after your enemy!

The Boots of the Gospel

Next, Paul tells us to have our *feet fitted with the readiness that comes from the gospel of peace*. In other words, we need to wear *the boots of the gospel*. Boots cover your feet—the parts of your body that move you from point *A* to point *B*. You mobilize and deploy on your feet. You pursue the enemy on your feet. When your commander sends you out from your base camp to your battlefield position, what does he give you? *Marching* orders! And you march on your feet.

When did our Warrior-King give us our marching orders? When He gave us the Great Commission in Matthew 28:19-20. The heart of the Great Commission is expressed in four simple words in verse 19: "Go and make disciples." Notice, especially, that first word: "Go!" Jesus, our Lord and Commander, gave us a commission, and the first word of that commission is "Go!" So our job is to put our boots on—the boots of the gospel, the boots of the story of Jesus Christ and the salvation He brings—and to go and take that gospel around the world, making disciples wherever we go.

So go fulfill the Great Commission. Lace up your boots and then go and make disciples.

The Shield of Faith

Next, Paul tells us to take up *the shield of faith*, with which we can extinguish all the flaming arrows of the evil one. In Paul's day, Roman legionnaires carried large rectangular shields made of wood covered with leather. The warriors could form a wall of shields, leaving no gap from one shield to the next. This wall of shields could not be penetrated even by the fire-tipped arrows of the enemy.

Faith, says Paul, is our shield against the flaming arrows of our enemy. What is faith? It is our trust and confidence in God and His promises. Faith is taking God at His word. Where does faith come from? Paul says, "So then faith comes by hearing, and hearing by the word of God" (Rom. 10:17, *NKJV*). The Lord gives us faith by means of His Word, the Bible. The more of His Word that we build into our lives, the stronger our shield of faith—and the more invulnerable we become to the enemy's flaming arrows of doubt, discouragement and temptation.

The Helmet of Salvation

Next, Paul tells us to take *the helmet of salvation*. Any soldier who goes into battle without his helmet is taking a foolish risk. A helmet covers the head, protecting the brain, the organ of thought. The helmet of salvation guards the warrior's thoughts and his will; it preserves his life. When the enemy attacks and tries to disrupt our thoughts and corrupt our will, we can rely upon our salvation to repel those attacks: "No matter how difficult my circumstances, no matter how I feel emotionally, no matter how Satan may attack me, I *know* that Jesus Christ is saving me right now. I put my trust in the helmet of my salvation."

The Sword of the Spirit

Next, Paul tells us to take *the sword of the Spirit*, which is the Word of God. Every other piece of equipment that Paul has talked about so far has been *defensive* armor. But a sword is an *offensive* weapon. It doesn't merely protect you; it slays your enemies. As the writer to the Hebrews said, "For the word of God is living and active. Sharper than any double-edged sword, it penetrates even to dividing soul and spirit, joints and marrow; it judges the thoughts and attitudes of the heart" (Heb. 4:12).

When Jesus was tempted in the desert, He engaged in exactly the same kind of spiritual warfare that you and I face. How did He defend Himself? By going on the offensive! He wielded His sword, the Word of God. Matthew 4 tells us that when Jesus was tempted by Satan, He was weak from 40 days of fasting. The enemy tempted Him to turn stones into bread, to test God by leaping from the highest pinnacle of the Temple, and to gain power by worshiping the prince of evil. Jesus answered each temptation with Scripture: "It is written . . . It is written . . . It is written . . ." (v. 4,7,10). Jesus didn't merely defend Himself; He went on the offensive. The result: "Then the devil left him" (v. 11).

The same thing happens when we go on the offensive, attacking Satan with the sword of the Spirit, the Word of God: "Resist the devil, and he will flee from you" (Jas. 4:7). That is what the sword is for: to put your enemy to flight! When you use your sword against Satan, you put the fear of God into him! You threaten him! So read the Word daily, study it and memorize it so that your sword is always ready for battle whenever the enemy shows his ugly face. As the psalmist said, "I have hidden your word in my heart that I might not sin against you" (Ps. 119:11).

The Communication Line of Prayer

Finally, Paul says *pray in the Spirit* on all occasions. Prayer is our communication line. Through prayer, we have instant access to our Commander-in-Chief. Whatever we need to carry out our mission and defeat our enemies is instantly available to us through prayer.

These defenses and weapons may not seem like much to our eyes—because they are not physical, not visible—but our enemy fears these weapons as if they were laser-guided smart bombs. God has been in the business of spiritual warfare for a long time. We may not always know what He's doing—but He does. Trust Him. Follow Him. Have confidence that He is working all things together for good in your life. Then go—and do your duty as His choice warrior.

THE BATTLEGROUND WITHIN

Where do you fight this war? On the spiritual battlefield of your heart and soul. The first battleground you must conquer is the battleground within. Put on the full armor of God and then battle for your integrity, your character, your faithfulness and your loyalty to God. Battle temptation, compromise and sin through the power of the Word and the power of prayer. Fight the good fight when you are tempted by thoughts of lust, by the easy but dishonest dollar, by the temptation to lose your cool with your kids. Right there, in the deepest places of your heart, be the righteous, virtuous warrior that your Lord and Commander calls you to be.

Whatever you do, don't let sin gain the victory over you. The warrior within must always be watchful of the enemy within. In *Wild at Heart*, John Eldredge says that there is a traitor within each of us. If we let our guard down, that traitor will surrender the castle of our souls to the enemy. Eldredge writes:

Stand on what is true and do not let go. Period. The traitor within the castle will try to lower the drawbridge but don't let him. . . . As Thomas à Kempis says, "Yet we must be watchful, especially in the beginning of the temptation; for the enemy is then more easily overcome, if he is not suffered to enter the door of our hearts, but is resisted without the gate at his first knock."[3]

Remember, spiritual warfare is not waged against flesh and blood. People may hate you, attack you and even try to kill you—but they are not your enemy. Your fight is against the invisible but intensely real demonic enemy who holds those people prisoner. When people hate you, don't hate back. Keep your weapons trained on your *real* enemy.

The next battlefield you face is all around you. Go out into the world with your boots laced for battle. Go into your office, your school, your neighborhood, your military base, your church. Be a gentle, compassionate warrior for God's truth and grace.

In 1655, a Scottish Christian named William Gurnall described the awe-inspiring ultimate outcome of the warfare that now engulfs us. In his book *The Christian in Complete Armour*, he wrote:

As part of Christ's army, you march in the ranks of gallant spirits. Every one of your fellow soldiers is the child of a King. Some, like you, are in the midst of the battle, besieged on every side by affliction and temptation. Others, after many assaults, repulses, and rallyings of their faith, are already standing upon the wall of heaven as conquerors. From there they look down and urge you, their comrades on earth, to march up the hill after them. This is their cry: "Fight to the death and the City is your own, as now it is ours! For the waging of a few days' conflict, you will be rewarded with heaven's glory."[4]

Don't let sin gain the victory over you. The warrior within must always be watchful of the enemy within.

The war we fight is no mere metaphor. It's the ultimate reality of our lives and of all eternity.

THE COURAGE OF A WARRIOR

Can a warrior ever be afraid? Of course he can. You can't say a man has courage if he has never known fear. Courage is *not* the absence of fear. Courage is *doing the thing you fear* because it's the right thing to do. In his book *Orthodoxy*, G. K. Chesterton described the paradox of courage:

> Courage is almost a contradiction in terms. It means a strong desire to live taking the form of a readiness to die. . . . [A man] can only get away from death by continually stepping within an inch of it. A soldier surrounded by enemies, if he is to cut his way out, needs to combine a strong desire for living with a strange carelessness about dying. He must not merely cling to life, for then he will be a coward, and will not escape. He must not merely wait for death, for then he will be a suicide, and will not escape. He must seek his life in a spirit of furious indifference to it; he must desire life like water and yet drink death like wine.[5]

The source of authentic Christian courage is *faith and confidence in an all-powerful God*. In 2 Chronicles 32, we read of a time when Jerusalem was about to be attacked by Sennacherib, the brutal, take-no-prisoners king of Assyria. Hezekiah, ruler of Judah (the southern kingdom of Israel), called his warriors together and gave them a speech about courage. "Be strong and courageous," he told them. "Do not be afraid or discouraged because of the king of Assyria and the vast army with him, for there is a greater power with us than with him. With him is only the arm of flesh, but with us is the LORD our God to help us and to fight our battles" (vv. 7-8).

The people of Judah gained confidence and courage from King Hezekiah's words. The Assyrian invasion ended with the destruction of Sennacherib's mighty army. The courage to face the brutal Assyrian army came from faith and confidence in an all-powerful God.

We see the same principle in the New Testament. In Acts 4, we see Peter and the other apostles of the Early Church being threatened, persecuted and imprisoned by the Sanhedrin, the religious elders of Israel. The apostles were the men who had walked with Jesus, the founders of the Early Church. When the Sanhedrin heard that the apostles were teaching about Jesus in the Temple courts, they sent guards to arrest the apostles.

As the apostles stood before the Sanhedrin, the high priest said, "We gave you strict orders not to teach in this name," meaning the name of Jesus. "Yet you have filled Jerusalem with your teaching and are determined to make us guilty of this man's blood" (Acts 5:28).

The apostles answered with words of invincible courage: "We must obey God rather than men! The God of our fathers raised Jesus from the dead—whom you had killed by hanging him on a tree" (vv. 29-30).

When you know that Almighty God is on your side, you don't worry about what your enemies might do to you. When your confidence is in Him, you have an inexhaustible supply of courage.

"Be on your guard," wrote the apostle Paul. "Stand firm in the faith; be men of courage; be strong" (1 Cor. 16:13). To Timothy, Paul said, "For God has not given us a spirit of fear, but of power and of love and of a sound mind" (2 Tim. 1:7, NKJV). And the writer to the Hebrews wrote, "But Christ is faithful as a son over God's house. And we are his house, if we hold on to our courage and the hope of which we boast" (Heb. 3:6).

A true warrior is a man of courage because he's a man of faith. He knows that when he dies, God will receive him and reward him with the words, "Well done, good and faithful servant! . . . Come and share your master's happiness!" (Matt. 25:21) When outnumbered, the warrior within is unperturbed. He knows that one courageous warrior plus God outnumbers any opposing army. When surrounded, he does not surrender. He rejoices that he is in a "target-rich environment."

Shakespeare's drama *King Henry V* describes the events surrounding the Battle of Agincourt in northern France on St. Crispin's Day, October 25, 1415. In that battle, part of the Hundred Years' War, the army of King Henry V of England was vastly outnumbered by the forces of Charles VI of France. In Act 4, Scene 3 of Shakespeare's play, King Henry faces his demoralized troops and delivers a moving speech that ends with these words:

We few, we happy few, we band of brothers;
For he today that sheds his blood with me
Shall be my brother; be he ne'er so vile,
This day shall gentle his condition:
And gentlemen in England now a-bed
Shall think themselves accursed they were not here,
And hold their manhoods cheap whiles any speaks
That fought with us upon Saint Crispin's day.

Hearing that speech from their king, this army of outnumbered Englishmen found new boldness and courage. In that moment, they became a band of brothers, an army of warriors, and they fought like men. History records that the Battle of Agincourt was a brutal, bloody mêlée, carried out with swords, hatchets and knives. When it was over, the French forces had suffered over 5,000 killed; the outnumbered English under Henry V lost just over 100 men. To this day, the Battle of Agincourt stands as a symbol of indomitable courage in the face of overwhelming odds.

Before the Battle of Agincourt, the British were outnumbered and defeated by fear and despair. After the battle, they were victorious. Where did those warriors find the courage to win the Battle of Agincourt?

They found their courage in the words of their king.

Do you need courage for the battles of your life? Then listen to the words of your King. Stand firm in the faith! Be strong! Be bold! God has not given you a spirit of fear, but of power, of love and of a sound mind! You are one of the Lord's brave warriors, a spiritual descendent of Asher himself! You are one of the few, the happy few, the band of brothers who wear the full armor of God!

You may die in battle—but so what? You've already settled the matter of your death. So go forth in the joy of the Lord. Fight with the courage of a true warrior of the King.

Victory was yours the moment you chose the right side.

Notes

1. John Eldredge, *Waking the Dead: The Glory of a Heart Fully Alive* (Nashville, TN: Nelson Books, 2003).
2. C. S. Lewis, *Mere Christianity* (SanFrancisco: HarperCollins, 2001).

3. John Eldredge, *Wild at Heart: Discovering the Secret of a Man's Soul* (Nashville, TN: Nelson Books, 2001).

4. William Gurnall, *The Christian in Complete Armour* (London: Banner of Truth Press, 1979).

5. G. K. Chesterton, *Orthodoxy* (Fort Collins, CO: Ignatius Press, 1995).

Raise a Generation of Warriors

I was 24 years old in September 1964 when I got my marching orders from Uncle Sam. I had signed up for the Army Reserves the previous year and now it was time to report for eight weeks of basic training. I went to Fort Jackson, South Carolina, and got my first taste of military life, courtesy of Sergeant Enrique Fishbach.

Sergeant Fishbach was a Cuban-American and a classic spit-and-polish drill sergeant. His jaw was like a concrete block, his eyes like ball-bearings, and he stood as straight as iron rebar. His boots were polished to a mirror-like finish. He had the kind of voice that was impossible to disobey. To this day, I can't think about Sergeant Fishbach without experiencing a twisting sensation in my innards. The Sergeant was a warrior.

There was another recruit in our unit, a fella named Don Wehde. Let me tell you, Don Wehde was no Sergeant Fishbach! Don was a 6' 4" disk jockey with a lot of charm, the life of the party—but he was definitely not Government Issue. Yet, for some strange reason known only to the powers-that-be, good old Don was elevated to squad leader.

Frankly, I don't think anyone was more astonished than Don. But he soon got over his astonishment. In fact, he quickly morphed into a real tough-as-nails Army squad leader! He started barking orders, kicking tail, marching us around the grounds, and chewing us out for every little infraction.

Well, for a few weeks, it was mighty unpleasant being in Don's squad. But then he did something that made Sergeant Fishbach mad. I don't know what it was, but it was big enough that Don got busted from squad leader back to grunt. It was a big relief that Don was one of the guys again.

I can still picture Don, marching along in the last row. I'll never forget the words he said when he came back to our ranks after getting busted:

"Well, men, I'm back—just bopping along with the troops!"

Now, flash forward 40 years. In January 2005, I was booked to do a radio interview about my book *Coaching Your Kids to Be Leaders*, which had just been released. In that book, I told the story of Don Wehde and our eight weeks at Fort Jackson. The radio interview would be broadcast over a Chicago radio station, originating as a live remote from Disney World in Orlando. I walked onto the set and the producer said, "You're going to be interviewed by radio host Don Wehde and his wife."

My jaw dropped. I said, "Is his name spelled W-E-H-D-E? Is he a big, tall fella?" The producer said yes and yes. I said, "What are the odds? He's in this book!"

So I walked onto the set and there was Don. I hadn't seen him in 40 years! Well, Don had remembered me from Fort Jackson, so when he came to Orlando, he brought his Army yearbook from basic training. We had a nice chat before going on the air, and we looked at all the pictures in the yearbook, including pictures of Sergeant Fishbach.

Finally, Don said, "Tell me about your new book."

"Don," I said, "you're in it! Your story is right here on page 269! I talked about you and Fort Jackson!"

All the color drained from his face. "What did you say about me?"

I opened the book and handed it to him. "Don," I said, "just read." He read—and then laughed. We went on the air live, and Don opened the show by saying, "Hey, folks! I'm in Pat Williams's new book!" We talked about our Fort Jackson days on the air.

It was clear that Don's Army experience had made a big impression on him. He may have joked about getting busted. He may have acted casual when he said he was "just bopping along with the troops." But for a while there, this happy-go-lucky deejay had been a real blood-and-guts warrior. Deep down, every man knows there's a warrior within him.

When I look around at kids today—my own kids, the kids in my church, the kids I speak to at various youth events—I can't help thinking of these two men from basic training at Fort Jackson. I can't help thinking of Sergeant Enrique Fishbach, the consummate Regular Army warrior—and Don Wehde, marching in the back of the ranks, just bopping along with the troops. Even good old Don had the stuff of a warrior in his soul.

When it comes to spiritual warfare, we need to raise up a generation of young Sergeant Fishbachs—Christian youth who will lay down their lives in service to Jesus, their Warrior-King. You may think that the kids in your family or your classroom or your youth group are just bopping along through life. But I'm betting there's a bit of Sergeant Fishbach inside each one. Your job is to turn boppers into warriors.

There are so many young people around us with warrior potential—and they're just waiting for someone to challenge them, motivate them, inspire them, put the spiritual weaponry in their hands, and point them to the battlefield. They could be spiritual warriors in their schools, on the playing field, in their homes and neighborhoods, in their churches—if only their parents, teachers or coaches would reach out to them.

Asher raised up a genealogy filled with 26,000 brave warriors ready for battle. Why shouldn't we do the same? Why shouldn't we raise up generations of brave spiritual warriors for God, ready to go to war against Satan, armored and trained and eager to put this ancient enemy to flight?

THE WORLD NEEDS YOUNG WARRIORS

Boys love playing war. They love to shoot, hack, stab, fall down dead, get up, and shoot-hack-stab some more. You can take away their violent toys and TV shows and preach peace and love to them all day long, but you can't stop them from playing war. Why? Because the aggression isn't in the toys they play with or the cartoons they watch. It's built into them. Little boys are hard-wired to play Capture the Flag and to shoot each other with squirt guns. In fact, it's *good* for them to play such games. They learn lessons in teamwork and strategy. They get exercise and sunshine.

Kids *want* a cause to fight for, a battle to win. They *want* to feel the power of warriorhood flowing through them. They *want* to spend their

Kids *want* to feel the power of warriorhood flowing through them. They *want* to spend their lives doing something that counts, something that has meaning.

lives doing something that counts, something that has meaning.

The world needs more young warriors like 15-year-old Danny Rohrbough. This high school freshman was a computer whiz who liked to help out his dad in the family electronics business. He was excitedly looking forward to getting his driver's permit. One warm spring day in 1999, Danny was eating lunch in the cafeteria at Columbine High School.

But then two male students showed up in black trenchcoats, firing at students and trying to set off a pair of butane bombs. Students screamed and ran for the doors. Danny Rohrbough was one of them—but once he made it outside, he turned around and went back. Why? He made a decision to hold the door open so more kids could escape.

One of the killers saw Danny holding the door, so he took aim and shot Danny three times. This brave young warrior fell to the sidewalk and died. He could have saved himself, but he stayed to save others.

This world needs more young warriors who are willing to stand at the bloody crossroads of history and hold open the door of life for their generation. If there were more young warriors like Danny Rohrbough in the world, we'd have fewer soul-dead killers like the boys who took his life.

You and I have a big challenge before us. We need to inspire and motivate the next generation of warriors. Our challenge is to raise up a generation of godly young warriors, spiritual descendents of Asher. We must teach them how to put on the whole armor of God so that they will be equipped and ready for the spiritual battles of life.

Our young warriors will get knocked down and wounded. That's what warfare is all about. They have to know that we are with them, rooting for them, cheering them on, win or lose. Let me tell you a pair of stories from the 1992 Barcelona Olympics to illustrate the point.

Derek Redmond of Great Britain was a brilliant runner—and a wounded warrior. By the time he reached Barcelona, his hopes for Olympic gold had already been frustrated once. In the 1988 Summer Olympics in Seoul, Korea, he had pulled an Achilles tendon in a qualifying heat for the 400-meter race. That injury resulted in five surgeries, the most recent surgery taking place just four months before Barcelona.

But when Derek stepped onto the track for the Barcelona Olympics, he felt good—and he ran well. After winning the quarterfinal heat, he got into the blocks for the semifinal. The starting gun split the air and Derek got off to a good, smooth start. He felt like it was his best run yet.

Then, a little more than a third of the way through the 400-meter race, pain lanced through Derek Redmond's right thigh. Suddenly, all the strength in that leg evaporated. He staggered and fell with a torn hamstring.

Trainers and stretcher-bearers rushed toward him to carry him off the track. Derek got up on his left leg and pushed everyone away. "No!" he said, "I have to finish!" Then Derek felt an arm around him and he heard a familiar voice say, "Derek, it's me!" Derek looked up—and saw his father, Jim Redmond.

Derek's dad was a big man with a white T-shirt that read HAVE YOU HUGGED YOUR CHILD TODAY? "You don't have to do this," Jim Redmond told his son.

"Yes, I do," Derek said, gritting his teeth. "I have to finish the race."

"If you're going to finish it," Jim said, "we'll finish it together."

So Derek Redmond, a wounded warrior, leaned on his father's shoulder, and they made their way toward the finish line, staying in Derek's lane all the way. A few meters before the end of the race, Jim released his grip on his son. Derek crossed the finish line on his own. The crowd of 65,000 people stood, cheered and wept. They had seen the naked heart of a warrior that day—and they had seen the reason why Derek Redmond had such a courageous heart. Jim Redmond was his father.

When our kids fall in battle, they need us to be there for them—not to fight their battles or carry them off the field. They just need us to be there to support them and walk alongside them for a while so that they can finish the job they came to do.

During the opening ceremonies of the 1992 Barcelona Olympics, athletes from all nations came out and carried their flags in the traditional parade around the field of competition. One of those athletes was swimmer Ron Karnaugh of Mapletown, New Jersey. Favored to win the gold in the 200-meter medley, Karnaugh was living the dream of a lifetime. As he walked along that track, he was amazed that he was able to spot his father up in the stands, calling his name and waving. "In a stadium with all those people," Ron later recalled, "what are the odds of that?"

A short time later, Ron's dream was overshadowed by tragedy. Immediately after the opening ceremonies, Ron's father, Peter, was climbing the stairs when he suffered a massive heart attack. He died a short time later.

It was a crushing emotional blow for Ron Karnaugh. This was supposed to be the crowning moment of his life. Instead, the 1992 games symbolized a crushing loss. Yet Ron Karnaugh was a warrior. He refused to surrender to his grief.

Five days after the death of his father, Ron Karnaugh arrived at the pool for the 200-meter medley. He wore his father's favorite hat—the hat that Peter Karnaugh had always worn when he and young Ron had gone fishing or boating together. By bringing his dad's hat to the event, Ron wasn't just paying tribute to his late father. He actually felt closer to his dad—as if a part of his dad's enthusiastic spirit was there at poolside with him.

Before the competition, Ron carefully set the hat aside. Then he took his place at the edge of the pool and competed like a true warrior. He didn't win the gold—nor even the silver or bronze. He placed sixth—a respectable but disappointing finish. Even so, Ron felt that his father's spirit was there beaming with pride.

The death of his dad had a profound impact on Ron Karnaugh; so did his mother's diagnosis with cancer of the larynx the following year. Those two tragedies convinced Ron Karnaugh to seek a career in medicine. They call him "Doctor Ron" today—thanks in large part to George Steinbrenner, owner of the New York Yankees and vice president of the U.S. Olympic Committee (1989-1996). Moved by Ron Karnaugh's loss, Steinbrenner picked up the tab for the young man's medical education.

Looking back, Ron is grateful for that one last glimpse of his dad just minutes before Peter Karnaugh's fatal heart attack. "It's almost like that's the way God wanted it to be," Ron told an interviewer for *Swimming World Magazine*. "For a year or two, it was really hard to cope with, thinking, 'Why me? And why did this happen at the Olympics?' . . . But having gone through med school, I see how people live and die every day, and I feel really grateful for the time I had with him."[1]

If you raise your children to be warriors, you can know that they will carry on the battle, even if you're not physically with them. When you raise a warrior, you become a part of his or her life that can never be erased.

THE EXAMPLE OF JESUS: HOW TO BUILD A WARRIOR

When people think of Jesus, they tend to think of Him as a preacher, teacher, healer and miracle worker. But look carefully at His life and you see that He was primarily a mentor. He spent much more time with the Twelve than He spent with the masses. He was mentoring and training the Twelve to be His foot-soldiers in a spiritual revolution. Jesus put them through intensive training sessions. He encouraged and taught them. He disciplined and confronted them. He often threw them into challenging situations.

As the Twelve learned and grew, He gradually placed more and more responsibility on their shoulders. That's the way mentoring works. First, the mentor says, "I'll work; you watch." Then he says, "I'll work; you help." Then he says, "You work; I'll help." Finally, he says, "You work; I'll watch."

In Matthew 10, we see the culmination of this process as Jesus gathers the Twelve to Himself and then sends them out with power, authority and a battle plan to wage spiritual warfare in His name. When Jesus began His ministry, He was just one warrior. By training the Twelve, He multiplied Himself twelve times over. Here's the five-part mentoring strategy of Jesus.

Part 1: Jesus Warned the Twelve of the Dangers They Faced

Jesus knew that His disciples were going out to a battlefield, and He prepared them for the hostile action they would face. "I am sending you out like sheep among wolves," He said. "Therefore be as shrewd as snakes and as innocent as doves" (v. 16).

The Warrior-King sent His disciples out into a hostile world as sheep among wolves—and that is what He calls us to do. As parents, pastors, youth workers, teachers, mentors and coaches, Jesus calls us to send our kids out into a dangerous world as sheep among wolves, as gentle warriors in a world that hates them.

That's not easy, is it? We want to protect our kids. We want to coddle them and keep their feelings from getting hurt. But as Dr. Tony Evans has said, "We must never be content with simply protecting our kids from the world. Rather, our goal should be to equip them to help change the world so that, when they go out into it, they do so as lights in the midst of darkness. If we do our parenting job right and they choose to walk with God, it won't be them so much as the world that's in trouble, because of the impact they'll make upon it."

Part 2: Jesus Inspired the Courage of the Twelve

Three times in Matthew 10, Jesus tells His disciples, "Do not be afraid" (see v. 26,28,31). He warns them that everything that has been done to Him will be done to them, because "a student is not above his teacher, nor a servant above his master" (v. 24). They will be hated, persecuted and betrayed—yet, just as He has shown courage in the face of opposition, they must be courageous as well.

As parents, teachers and mentors, we need to build the courage and boldness of our young warriors. We need to encourage them to take risks and attempt "impossible" tasks. Let them know that if they do great things, they will make enemies. They'll be hated, persecuted and betrayed. But encourage them to do great things anyway. Cheer them when they win and encourage them when they fail. Tell them, "Don't be afraid! You're a warrior!"

Part 3: Jesus Gave His Disciples Authority to Act in His Name

The Bible tells us, "[Jesus] called his twelve disciples to him and gave them authority." (v. 1). He didn't just lecture them in the classroom. He sent them out with power to do ministry on His behalf.

As we raise, train and mentor kids to be warriors, we need to give them authority. We need to give them the power to make their own

As we raise, train and mentor kids to be warriors, we need to give them the power to make their own decisions—and that means letting them make their own mistakes!

decisions—and that means letting them make their own mistakes! They won't learn to be warriors if we only lecture them in the classroom. They need battlefield experience, so we must send them into battle with authority to take action. Let them earn a few Purple Hearts. Let them earn the right to call themselves warriors.

Part 4: Jesus Placed Costly Demands on the Twelve

Jesus commanded His disciples' loyalty and demanded their sacrifice. He said: "Whoever acknowledges me before men, I will also acknowledge him before my Father in heaven. But whoever disowns me before men, I will disown him before my Father in heaven. . . . Anyone who loves his father or mother more than me is not worthy of me; anyone who loves his son or daughter more than me is not worthy of me; and anyone who does not take his cross and follow me is not worthy of me" (vv. 32-33,37-38).

If we want to raise generations of warriors, as Asher did, then we must challenge our kids to live lives of sacrifice and self-denial. This is all-out, take-no-prisoners spiritual warfare. Our young people need to see themselves as soldiers living under battlefield conditions. Instead of reducing the demands to make it easy on our kids, we should raise the demands and cheer them on as they accept the challenge.

Part 5: Jesus Prepared the Twelve for Battle

Jesus told His disciples, in effect, "This is war!" He said, "Do not suppose that I have come to bring peace to the earth. I did not come to bring peace, but a sword. For I have come to turn 'a man against his father, a daughter against her mother, a daughter-in-law against her mother-in-law—a man's enemies will be the members of his own household'" (vv. 34-36). Jesus didn't want His disciples to think for a moment that they were civilians or innocent bystanders. They were warriors. This is a message we must get across to our young warriors as well.

In commissioning the Twelve to be His warriors, waging spiritual warfare in His name, Jesus made this promise: "I tell you the truth, anyone who has faith in me will do what I have been doing. He will do even greater things than these, because I am going to the Father" (John 14:12). It's true: Jesus multiplied Himself times twelve; then the Twelve multiplied themselves many times over; and the multiplication continued, generation after generation. The followers of Jesus did greater things than Jesus Himself; they carried on the war, attacking Satan's strongholds, establishing new battlefronts, taking new territory, winning battle after battle, even after the Warrior-King Himself had returned to the Father.

Your job and mine is to continue training new warriors and sending them into battle. We must inspire and motivate them to expand the front lines and push into new territory. We are the old warriors who are bringing up the next generation of spiritual soldiers. Our job is to remind them that this is not a war of hate, death or destruction. It's a war of truth, righteousness and obedience to our Lord and Commander.

As that tough old warrior, the apostle Paul, once wrote, "For though we live in the world, we do not wage war as the world does. The weapons we fight with are not the weapons of the world. On the contrary, they have divine power to demolish strongholds" (2 Cor. 10:3-4).

HOW TO PRAY FOR YOUR YOUNG WARRIORS

One of the most effective ways to raise spiritual warriors is by praying for them. I can tell you of my own personal knowledge that God can move human hearts, including the hearts of stubborn and rebellious children, through the power of prayer alone. When nothing else can reach a child, *God can*—through the prayers of faithful, godly parents. We should pray for them daily, regularly and specifically. Here are some specific requests to lay before God as you pray for your young warriors.

If your kids don't have a relationship with God, or if you're unsure, pray that they will come to a personal relationship with Him. If your kids already have a faith-relationship with God, express your thanks to Him and ask Him to deepen your kids' faith.

Pray for grace to set a godly example to your kids. Ask for the right words to say and for the wisdom and boldness to speak up. Pray that God would inspire you to be a model of godly character, patience, forgiveness and faith.

Ask God to give your kids a sense of calling and purpose in their lives—a desire to serve God and others.

Pray that God will refine and purify your kids' character so that they will increasingly demonstrate the fruit of the Spirit (see Gal. 5:22-23).

Ask God to help your kids to reject the moral relativism of the world around them and to develop a healthy, moral Christian worldview. Ask Him to protect your kids from the pressures and pitfalls of youth culture today—drugs, alcohol, violence, sexual immorality and suicide.

Meditate in passages of Scripture that deal with prayer. As you read through the passage, pray those words back to God. For example, read through this passage from Paul's letter to the Philippians:

> And this is my prayer: that your love may abound more and more in knowledge and depth of insight, so that you may be able to discern what is best and may be pure and blameless until the day of Christ, filled with the fruit of righteousness that comes through Jesus Christ—to the glory and praise of God (Phil. 1:9-11).

As you read through this passage, you can pray these words back to the Lord on behalf of your children: "Lord, this is my prayer for my kids: Please let Your love abound more and more in their lives. Give my children increasingly more knowledge and depth of insight into Your truth so that they may be able to discern what is best and may be pure and blameless until the day of Christ. Lord, fill their lives with the fruit of righteousness that comes through Jesus Christ, and I will give you all the glory and the praise."

Here are some other excellent passages that you might want to pray through as you intercede on behalf of your children: Colossians 1:9-12; 3:12-17; Ephesians 1:15-19; 3:14-19; 4:12-15; 6:19-20; Philemon 1:6.

Finally, pray that your children will be faithful prayer warriors—that they would daily seek fellowship with God, presenting their requests to Him and seeking His guidance. Prayer is the secret weapon of the spiritual warrior. No one should go into battle without spending time alone with his Lord and Commander.

THE RIGHT BATTLES, THE RIGHT MASTER, THE RIGHT CAUSE

In December 1776, the fate of America hung by the slimmest of threads. General George Washington's makeshift army had suffered a series of humiliating and costly battlefield defeats. At the Battle of Long Island in late August, the Redcoats under General Howe had inflicted heavy losses on the Americans. The British pursued Washington's army through New Jersey, across the Delaware River, and into Pennsylvania.

Washington's forces had shrunk from 17,000 soldiers to a mere 3,000 exhausted and underfed men, some without coats or shoes to protect them from the harsh winter. When the Continental Congress in Philadelphia learned that General Washington had retreated to a place just 12 miles away, they panicked and fled to Baltimore, 100 miles to the south. From his camp near the Falls of Trenton, a dispirited General Washington wrote his brother John, "I think the game is pretty near up."

Washington needed a victory. One more battlefield loss and his army would be disbanded. His last hope—and America's—lay across the Delaware River in the sleepy town of Trenton, New Jersey.

The town was guarded by Hessian mercenaries—soldiers imported from Germany to fight for the British. The Hessians were commanded by Colonel Johann Gottlieb Rall, a vile, hard-drinking man without conscience or honor. During a battle in New York, Colonel Rall had ordered his soldiers to slaughter surrendering Americans.

General Washington gambled that the poorly disciplined Hessians would be so hungover after celebrating Christmas that Trenton would fall into his hands like an overripe plum. On Christmas Day, Washington divided his meager forces into three units. Washington would lead the largest group, roughly 2,000 men, across the Delaware at McKonkey's Ferry, nine miles north of Trenton. The other two groups would cross the river at points further south. As Washington and his men marched toward McKonkey's Ferry, some wore rags in place of boots. Their footsteps left a trail of blood.

The crossing of the river began at two in the afternoon. It took 14 hours to move all of Washington's men, horses and light cannons across the Delaware. A heavy sleet storm and large ice floes made the passage treacherous and miserable. It was well after 3 A.M. when the entire force was finally safe on the New Jersey side.

A British loyalist spotted Washington's army and sent a handwritten warning by messenger to the Hessians. The messenger hurried to Trenton

and delivered the message to Colonel Rall. The colonel, who was playing cards with his aides, tucked the message into his pocket without
reading it.

Meanwhile, General Washington rode at the head of his troops on a
nine-mile march toward Trenton. Unfortunately, most of his soldiers' mus-
kets had been soaked by the storm. Although a few infantrymen still had
dry powder for their guns, most would have to attack with bayonets alone.

Washington's army reached Trenton at 8 A.M., catching the Hessian
guards drunk and sleeping at their posts. Riding out in front of his troops,
General Washington shouted, "March on, my brave fellows! After me!"
And he turned his horse and led his men into the thick of the battle.

Hearing shouts and gunfire, an astonished Colonel Rall staggered out
into the streets. "What is this?" he shouted in German. Moments later, he
was felled by a gunshot. His men carried him into the Queen Street
Methodist Church, where he died. One of his men noticed the corner of a
note sticking out of the colonel's pocket. The man opened the note and
read: *The American army is marching on Trenton.*

The Hessians took heavy losses—more than 200 dead and wounded—
and quickly surrendered. The Americans suffered only 4 casualties and
took nearly 1,000 Hessian prisoners. The course of the war was completely changed that day, and America exists as a free nation because of George
Washington's daring gambit at Trenton.

The moral of the story: If you want to produce a generation of warriors, then you must exemplify what it means to be a warrior. You can't
push warriors into battle from behind. You must ride out in front of your
troops and call to them, "March on, my brave fellows! After me!" You
must turn your horse and ride into the thick of the battle.

You've probably heard of a young American named John Phillip
Walker Lindh, also known as "The American Taliban." After the
September 11 terrorist attacks, the United States invaded Afghanistan

---

If you want to produce a generation of warriors, then you
must exemplify what it means to be a warrior.

to shut down the terrorist training camps and overthrow the Taliban regime. John Walker Lindh was captured in Afghanistan on November 25, 2001. When he was found, he had a bullet wound in his upper-right thigh and was huddled in a basement bunker with terrorists from Pakistan, Uzbekistan and Saudi Arabia. Why was an American fighting on the side of terrorists?

Born to Frank Lindh and Marilyn Walker in 1981, John Walker Lindh was baptized Catholic but converted to Islam at age 16. He later traveled to Yemen to learn Arabic, and then to Pakistan, where he studied Islam at a *madrassa* (Islamic school). In the spring of 2001, he went to Afghanistan, where he trained at Osama bin Laden's training camp. After completing his training, he became a member of Al Ansar, a bin Laden fighting unit. After his capture in late 2001, he admitted being a fighter for al-Qaeda.

In February 2002, John Walker Lindh was indicted on federal charges. He accepted a plea agreement that reduced his sentence from life to 20 years without parole. He is currently serving his sentence in a federal prison in Victorville, northeast of Los Angeles.

John Walker Lindh wanted to be a warrior. Instead, he became a terrorist. Today, he's a prisoner. What went wrong in this young man's life?

In a *National Review* column, opinion writer Rob Long suggested an explanation: overindulgent, permissive parenting that failed to give him guidance when he was 16 and searching for meaning in his life. Long described Lindh as:

> The product of divorced parents from Marin County, California
> . . . raised in the very crucible of cultural nuttiness . . . a child
> of hot tubs, massage therapy, cultural relativism, amicable
> divorce, racial guilt, vegan diets, Chardonnay anti-Americanism,
> and 'Teach Peace' bumper stickers . . . a rich American kid
> from a rich American town who was raised to believe that every
> crazy idea and loony impulse he ever had was valid . . . and that
> America is a pretty bad place.[2]

The boy's parents never discouraged his fascination with Islam. In fact, they supported it. They financed his trips to Yemen and Pakistan. They paid his tuition at the Islamic schools he attended. An article in *Time* quoted his father Frank as telling his son, "I don't think you've really converted to Islam as much as you've found it within yourself; you sort of found your inner Muslim."[3]

When John Walker Lindh's parents divorced in 1999, the young man (then 18) dropped his father's last name and called himself by his mother's maiden name, Walker. As Rob Long concluded:

> I think there's something in that, the whole I-hate-Dad's-name thing. I know the divorce was probably really amicable and Marin County-ish, and that everyone was probably really cool about the whole thing, and that his dad never hassled him for his beliefs and incipient treason, but maybe . . . it's easier to hate a dad who refuses to hassle you about anything. Maybe you drop his name and change your religion and fly off to Yemen and fight for a filthy, evil government not because you're on any kind of 'spiritual journey,' as some of John Walker's relatives have suggested, but because you want your dad to drag you home [and] to slap some sense into you.[4]

As dads, teachers, coaches, youth workers and mentors, we need to love our kids enough to struggle with them, argue with them, and endure their confused rage. When they start moving in the wrong direction, we need to care enough to grab them by the nape of the neck and tell them, "I love you too much to let you ruin your life."

We don't let our kids go off and find their inner Muslim, their inner gang member, their inner sex addict, their inner meth head. We tell them, "I see something powerful and noble in you. I see a warrior within you. I see a young person made in God's image, with the capacity to make a godly difference in this world." We teach them how to fight the good fight of faith and then lead the way to the battle. We teach them to serve the right master and give their loyalty to the right cause. It's not enough to be a warrior. Warriors must serve the right cause or they are nothing but terrorists.

In this world, which has far too many terrorists and jihadists, trench-coat killers and gang-bangers, we need to be fathers and mentors like Asher. We need to raise up generations of Christian heads of families, choice Christian men, outstanding Christian leaders, and brave Christian warriors, ready for battle, equipped for spiritual warfare. If we fail to raise up warriors, then we have already lost the war.

God has declared war on the rulers, authorities and powers of this dark world, against the spiritual forces of evil that are all around us. Surrender is not an option. For the sake of Jesus Christ and His kingdom, for the sake of our kids and their eternal souls, this is a war we must fight and win—in our generation and in generations to come.

Notes

1. Kari Lydersen, "Doctor Ron," *Swimming World Magazine,* November 1997. http://www.swimmingworldmagazine.com/articles/swimmingworld/articles/199711-01sw_art.asp (accessed November 2005).

2. Rob Long, "Free to Go Bad: John Walker Lindh, an American Tragedy," *National Review,* December 31, 2001.

3. Timothy Roche, Brian Bennett, Anne Berryman et al., "The Making of John Walker Lindh, *Time,* September 29, 2002.

4. Long, "Free to Go Bad: John Walker Lindh, an American Tragedy."

DIMENSION 4:
LEADERSHIP

IMAGINE A LEADER . . .

The war council of the tribes was held in the tent of Zebulun on the grassy plain before Mount Tabor. Zebulun's gaunt face was red with anger as he shook his bony forefinger in Asher's face. "Your plan is madness!" he shouted. "I'll not give my sons to die in this fool's gambit!"

All around the tent, the other tribal leaders shifted uncomfortably. They knew that Asher was a choice man of proven judgment, but none had the nerve to confront Zebulun.

Asher, meanwhile, sat calmly while Zebulun spent his fury. Though Asher's face was lined and creased, though his hair and beard were gray, his eyes were as keen as ever. Asher commanded respect.

"If you are finished—" Asher began.

"I am not!" Zebulun snapped. "I ask you, how many warriors can we place upon the battlefield? A few thousand at best. And how many Amalekite warriors are camped upon the plain against us?"

"Our scouts say 20,000," Asher said. "Maybe more."

"Twenty thousand!" Zebulun threw his hands in the air in a gesture of frustration—though, to Asher, it seemed more like a gesture of surrender.

"All I hear from you, Zebulun," Asher said evenly, "is talk of retreat—and defeat. It's true we're outnumbered, but we are not outmatched. There is more to an army's strength than numbers alone."

"What's that supposed to mean?" Zebulun asked sourly.

"My sons have been watching the Amalekite troop movements," Asher said. "They'll report here before sundown. Then we'll have a better idea of the true strength of our enemy. Until then, I say we should maintain our faith in God Most High and prepare to drive the enemy out of our land."

Zebulun waggled his bony finger again. "I say we withdraw our forces across the river and concentrate our strength at the fording places. Yes, we would be yielding the plain to the Amalekites, but at least we could hold the river against them."

"For how long?" asked Asher. "If the Amalekites smell fear, they will bring more warriors against us and wipe us out. We cannot afford to wait.

We have to defeat them decisively, here and now."

"Father," said a deep voice at the flap of the tent.

All eyes turned.

A young men in armor stepped into the tent. He was in his late twenties, tall and lean, with an angular face. He held his war helmet in the crook of his arm and wore a sword at his side. "I hope I'm not interrupting," he said.

Asher beamed with pride. "Most of you know my third-born son, Ishvi," he said. "What news do you bring, my son?"

Ishvi's eyes flashed. "I have come from the camps of my brothers, Imnah and Ishvah. During the night, they raided the enemy's outposts and killed some of the Amalekites. The enemy hardly put up a struggle. Though they are many, they're exhausted from the march over the Aruna Pass. Even their horses are dusty and spiritless. Imnah says the time to attack is now."

"What about their numbers?" Zebulun said sharply. "There are 20,000 Amalekite warriors camped on the plain!"

"I think our earlier estimates were low," Ishvi said. "My brother Ishvah has a keen eye, and he thinks there are closer to 30,000 warriors."

Zebulun's jaw dropped. For the first time that day, he was speechless.

Asher grinned. "Ishvi," he said, "where is your brother Beriah? He was supposed to report to—"

"I'm here, Father," said a strong voice at the door of the tent.

Beriah stepped inside—and he dragged a wretched-looking prisoner along with him. Beriah was shorter and more stoutly built than Ishvi, but he was just as hard-muscled. His hair was a thick, black mane like that of a lion. He, too, wore battle armor and a sword, and he carried his helmet in one hand. The prisoner's hands were bound.

"My youngest son, Beriah," Asher said, introducing his son to the tribal leaders. "So, Beriah, you have brought a prisoner."

"A deserter, Father," Beriah said. "You can see the condition he's in— sick, weak and hungry. He says they were forced to march for days on half rations. Their captains flogged them to keep them moving. They've no stomach for fighting."

"It's just as Imnah and Ishvah said," Ishvi added. "If we attack now, the Amalekites will run."

Asher looked around the tent. "You've heard my sons' report. You've seen the wretched state of this Amalekite deserter. What do you say? Shall we drive these godless blasphemers out of our land—or shall we retreat?"

"Drive them out!" said one tribal leader. "Attack now!" said another. "Fight!" said another. Again and again, the answer was the same.

Finally, all the tribal delegates had spoken but one. Zebulun eyed Asher for a long time in silence. Then he spoke.

"Forgive me, Asher," Zebulun said in rasping voice. "You were right. I was wrong. My sons and I are with you. We will drive them out."

They launched the attack at dawn.

Be an Outstanding Leader

The first and most influential model of leadership in my life was my dad, Jim Williams. He was a teacher, a coach and a leader in the community where we lived. He was, above all, a leader in our home.

A little over a year after Dad returned home from World War II, my parents were expecting their fourth child. In February 1947, my sister Mary Ellen arrived. She was born mentally retarded. In those days, her condition was called "mongoloidism," but today we know it as Down Syndrome.

In those days, there was a stigma to having a mentally retarded child in the family. It was viewed as a biological failure on the part of the parents, and families tended to be very private about such matters. There were few places a family could turn to for information or support. There was very little research being done on behalf of kids with special needs. Mom and Dad asked themselves, "Why couldn't the community come together to find solutions to this problem?"

My dad had a vision for changing the way people looked at mental retardation. He and my mom did media interviews, led fund-raising events, and worked hard to educate the community. Dad met with his friend Bob Carpenter, owner of the Philadelphia Phillies, and together they founded an annual event, the Delaware All-Star High School Football Game (The Blue-Gold Game). The first game was held in 1956, and the event continues to this day, benefiting the Delaware Foundation for Retarded Children.

Dad didn't spend a lot of time preaching leadership to me. Leadership was just something he did. As I watched his example, I accepted it that leadership is simply what responsible people do. The pattern in the Asher household was probably like that of the Williams household. The descendants of Asher were outstanding leaders because Asher was a leadership role model. Asher probably didn't have to preach leadership to his kids and grandkids. Leadership was just something Asher did. He set an example, and his descendents absorbed his leadership model by osmosis.

I'M A LEADER!

From the time I was knee-high to a dugout bench, I've been passionate about sports. Youth sports was my training ground for leadership. I got to take the leadership lessons I absorbed at home from my dad and apply those lessons on the playing field. In high school and college, every position I played was a leadership position. In basketball, I was the point guard; in football, the quarterback; in baseball, the catcher. Although I was a leader, I never gave much thought to what leadership means. No adult ever taught me the principles of leadership.

In 1960, during my junior year at Wake Forest University in North Carolina, I had an experience that transformed my understanding of leadership. In fact, that one experience probably set the course of my career as a leader in professional sports.

Every November, Wake Forest held a big freshman-versus-varsity basketball game at the Winston-Salem Coliseum. Five days before the game was to take place, the president of our lettermen's club, Jerry Steele, said to me, "Williams, I'm volunteering you to put this game on. You're in charge."

"In charge of what?" I asked.

"Everything." And he meant *everything*. Nobody had done Thing One to make that game happen. So far, there was no publicity, no halftime show, and the tickets hadn't even been printed. I wanted to decline Jerry's gracious invitation, but I couldn't bring myself to say no. You see, at 6' 8" and 240 pounds, Jerry had a very persuasive personality.

For the next five days, I worked my tail off. I sent publicity information out to the local radio, TV and newspaper outlets. I called up a local high school band and put together a half-time show. I found a singer for the national anthem. I brought in cheerleaders. I learned how to delegate, give orders, run meetings and organize people to focus on a goal. In fact, I did just about all the things I would later do in my career as an NBA executive.

The night of the game came and everything happened on schedule. I got accolades from the athletics director, the coach, the players and the students. Even Jerry Steele said I did a great job—and he had only assigned the task to me because he knew it couldn't be done!

That night, I went to bed with a startling thought spinning in my brain: *Hey! I'm a leader!*

The Seven Dimensions of Leadership

What does it mean to be a leader?

In my book *The Magic of Teamwork*, I identify seven essential components or dimensions of effective leadership.[1] I derived these seven leadership ingredients from my study of the life of the greatest leader who ever lived, Jesus of Nazareth. I have gone on to explore that seven-part leadership model in my books *The Paradox of Power*[2] and *Coaching Your Kids to Be Leaders*. I have given hundreds of leadership talks around the country to business, sports and religious groups. From the response I've received, I've become firmly convinced that these are truly the essential dimensions of authentic leadership:

1. Vision
2. Communication
3. People Skills
4. Good Character
5. Competence
6. Boldness
7. Servanthood

Without question, Asher must have had each of these qualities in abundance. Only a man who was complete in all seven of these dimensions of leadership could have produced generations of descendents whom the Bible would call "outstanding leaders."

If you want to be a father and grandfather and great-grandfather of outstanding leaders, then you must be an outstanding leader yourself. The good news about leadership is that it's not something you're born with. It's a set of skills you can learn. You can learn to become more visionary, to communicate more persuasively, to work more effectively with people, and to be more competent and excellent at what you do. You can choose to demonstrate a more Christlike character, to be bolder and more courageous, to take bigger risks through faith in God, and to become more of a servant to others. As you become the leader God wants you to be, you also become a leadership model to your kids.

So let's take a walk through these seven crucial leadership dimensions and find out what authentic leadership is all about.

1. Vision

Every leader must have a vision. A leader who sees the invisible can inspire his followers to do the impossible. When your team can see your vision for the future, they have something to shoot for and sacrifice for. They know exactly what success will look like, because you've given them a vision of success.

Vision always precedes achievement. My friend Dr. Jay Strack, founder of Student Leadership University, has a mixed Latin-Spanish term for vision: *carpe mañana*, which means (so he says) "take hold of tomorrow." He explains, "A leader is one who sees the invisible. He looks further down the road than anyone else, because of forward thinking. He sees the big picture with wide-angle vision."

A vision is a word picture that describes a desirable future. When the leader's dream becomes the shared dream of the entire organization, miracles happen. People work together, synergize and achieve the impossible.

If there were no visionary leaders, the future would look just like the past. There would be no innovation, no progress, no change. Without the

As you become the leader God wants you to be, you also become a leadership model to your kids.

vision of Walt Disney, there would be no Disneyland or Walt Disney World. Without the vision of John F. Kennedy, we would not have landed men on the moon. Without the vision of Ronald Reagan and Pope John Paul II, Berlin would still be a divided city and Poland would still be an Iron Curtain country. Vision changes the world.

A vision should be clear and simple. In the Old Testament, God said, "Write this. Write what you see. Write it out in big block letters so that it can be read on the run" (Hab. 2:2, *THE MESSAGE*). In other words, make your vision so big, simple and memorable that it can be grasped at a glance.

A vision should be visual. It should create pictures in people's minds. In communicating your vision, use word pictures and colorful metaphors. Use object lessons and images. Let your vision be visual and visible.

A vision should require sacrifice. Leaders must inspire followers to pay the price of achieving a vision. "If your vision doesn't cost you something," said leadership guru John C. Maxwell, "it's only a daydream."

A vision should involve the emotions and inspire optimism. It should be exhilarating and upbeat. "There is no such thing as an emotionless vision," says Andy Stanley, founding pastor of Atlanta's North Point Community Church and author of *Visioneering*. "Vision is always accompanied by strong emotion, and the clearer the vision, the stronger the emotion."[3]

A vision should be a huge challenge, daunting, intimidating and audacious in its scope. When you unveil your vision, your followers should gasp in amazement. A vision should lift people's eyes from the ground to the skies of limitless possibility.

Dr. Robert Jarvik is the inventor of the first permanently implantable artificial heart and a visionary in the field of medicine. He once said, "Leaders are visionaries with a poorly developed sense of fear and no concept of the odds against them. They make the impossible happen."

As parents and teachers, we must help our kids uncork their imaginations and envision their own limitless potential. That is what Jesus, the Ultimate Visionary, did for His disciples, and especially for a man named Simon Peter. When Jesus first met him, Simon was an impetuous, unreliable fisherman. But Jesus had a vision for Simon's future, so he gave Simon a new name: "Peter," meaning "The Rock." Despite his new name, Peter was anything *but* a rock! Again and again, Jesus had to reprimand

Peter for his impulsiveness and empty braggadocio. In the hours before the crucifixion, Peter denied Jesus three times—even sealing his denial with a terrible oath.

Yet Jesus' vision of Peter never wavered. He forgave Peter and reinstated him. In the end, the Lord's vision of Peter won out over Peter's unstable tendencies. In the book of Acts and the two New Testament letters that bear his name, we see that Peter ultimately became the wise, stable, dependable leader that Jesus had envisioned all along.

But before a fisherman named Simon could become a leader named Peter, Jesus had to envision something that wasn't there. Jesus had to see "The Rock" in Peter when there was nothing but shifting sand. Jesus didn't settle for what people were. He envisioned what they could become. That's the kind of vision you and I must see when we look at our kids' lives.

2. Communication

It's not enough to have a vision. A leader must be able to communicate his vision to the team. "Leaders are great talkers," said management trainer Tom Peters. "Leadership takes an almost bottomless supply of verbal energy. . . . You can't be a leader these days and be the strong, silent type."

In early 2001, baseball manager Jim Tracy came to an Orlando Magic home game. He had just been hired as manager of the Los Angeles Dodgers, so I asked him his philosophy of leadership. "Communication is the key," Jim replied. "You can have the greatest vision in the world, but if you can't get it across to your team, what good is it?"

Two thousand years ago, Jesus had a vision of something He called "the kingdom of heaven." Everywhere He went, He talked about that vision. He described it in stories, word pictures, and metaphors. "The kingdom of heaven is like a man who sowed good seed in his field" (Matt. 13:24). "The kingdom of heaven is like yeast" (v. 33). "The kingdom of heaven is like treasure hidden in a field" (v. 44). He compared the kingdom of heaven to a fishing net (see v. 47), a landowner (see 20:1) and a mustard seed (see Mark 4:30).

Jesus was not just a new kind of leader—he was a new kind of communicator. He showed us how to lead by energizing people with words. "My sheep listen to my voice," He said. "I know them, and they follow me" (John 10:27). That's our goal as leaders and communicators. We want our kids to listen to us and follow us, as we follow the Good Shepherd.

3. People Skills

Leaders must have people skills in order to lead. They must know how to listen, inspire, motivate, manage conflict and build teams. A "leader" without people skills is nothing but a boss.

A boss focuses on getting results; a leader with people skills focuses on building relationships. A boss focuses on maintaining his own power; a leader focuses on empowering others. Bosses trust only themselves; leaders say, "I have confidence in you." Bosses fear the successes of others; leaders achieve success *through* others. Bosses intimidate; leaders motivate. Bosses criticize weakness; leaders affirm strengths.

A leader with authentic people skills focuses on future successes, not past failures. Sure, leaders must sometimes confront, and confrontation is never easy. But if a leader spends 98 percent of his time affirming and building people up, he'll earn the right to be blunt and tough the other 2 percent of the time.

I recently had a talk with entrepreneur Howard Schultz. He bought a little coffee company called Starbucks and expanded it from 3 coffeehouses in 1987 to almost 10,000 stores today. A few years ago, Howard bought the Seattle Supersonics for $250 million. I asked him, "In a company the size of Starbucks, where do your leaders come from?"

"We are opening new stores at a rate of four a day," he told me. "We have to invest a lot of time and money in leadership training. We have to find our leaders within the company. You can't find the Starbucks culture outside of the company, so we must train from within."

"How do you spot leaders?" I asked.

"People skills!" he said. "To be a leader at Starbucks, you must have people skills. That's what our business is all about."

On March 20, 2005, I coached third base for the National League team in the Major League Baseball Alumni game in Clearwater, Florida.

Wade Boggs played third base for the American League. Boggs, of course, is remembered primarily for his years as a third baseman with the Boston Red Sox. His hitting dominated the American League during the 1980s and '90s. The most difficult year of his career was 1986, when his mother, Sue, was killed in a car accident. During the game, I asked Boggs which of his managers had the biggest impact on his life. Without hesitating, he said, "John McNamara, because he helped me get through the death of my mother."

John McNamara, who guided the Sox to the 1986 World Series, had a special people skill. He had a gift—call it compassion, empathy or mercy—that helped Wade Boggs work through his grief. That's one of the rarest, most valuable and most *human* people skills a leader can have.

4. Character

John Baldoni, author of *Personal Leadership*, stated the relationship between leadership and character this way: "Leadership is rooted in character. Character is defined as the sum of the attributes that form who a person is."[4] And the poet Ralph Waldo Emerson said, "Every great institution is the lengthened shadow of a single man. His character determines the character of his organization."

This world has plenty of bosses, chiefs, honchos and big kahunas—people with plenty of power but little character. We desperately need more choice men in the Asher mold—leaders with authentic character.

5. Competence

Dr. J. Richard Chase, former president of Biola University, said, "If a leader demonstrates competency, genuine concern for others, and admirable character, people will say, 'I like what that person is doing. I'm going to follow him.'" And John C. Maxwell said, "Competence goes beyond words. It's the leader's ability to say it, plan it, and do it in such a way that others know that you know how—and know that they want to follow you."

Another word for "competence" is "excellence." Competent people produce excellent work. As leaders we should set an example of excellence in everything we do. We should preach excellence, expect excellence and promote that warm feeling of accomplishment that comes from a job well done. Never let kids get away with a halfway effort. Tell them, "Try it again. I know you can achieve much more when you aim for excellence."

As the apostle Paul said, "Whatever you do, work at it with all your heart, as working for the Lord, not for men" (Col. 3:23). As missionary and Olympic athlete Eric Liddle said in the motion picture *Chariots of Fire*, "God made me fast. And when I run, I feel his pleasure." That godly pleasure comes when we demonstrate excellence and competence, stretching our efforts to the limits of our ability.

6. Boldness

If you're not bold, you're not a leader! Leaders can't afford to play it safe. As Florida State University coach Bobby Bowden says, "The Bible teaches us to 'fear not.' That's a good starting point for any aspiring leader." And the apostle Paul wrote, "For God did not give us a spirit of timidity, but a spirit of power, of love and of self-discipline" (2 Tim. 1:7).

Walt Disney often risked everything he had on an idea. The Disney empire walked a financial tightrope throughout much of Walt's career. If he hadn't been a bold and courageous leader, we never would have had *Snow White and the Seven Dwarfs*, *Fantasia* or Disneyland. Walt once said, "The main quality of leadership is courage. If you can dream it, you can do it."

Boldness isn't just the key to success in business. It's also the key to effective ministry for Jesus Christ. In the summer of 1978, while I was general manager of the Philadelphia 76ers, we acquired forward Bobby Jones from the Denver Nuggets. Bobby was a big factor in the 76ers' championship run in 1983—but he was an even bigger factor in the team's moral character.

Bobby Jones was the spiritual leader. The 6' 9" North Carolinian never drank, smoked or swore. The only time Bobby ever argued with an official was when the ref called a foul on another player. In his soft-spoken way, Bobby said, "Sir, that foul was on me." Normally quiet and reserved, Bobby's face came alight whenever he spoke about Jesus Christ.

Soon after joining the 76ers, Bobby came to me with a bold new idea. "Pat," he said, "I'd like to see the team have a chapel before each game."

"A chapel?"

"Yeah. A short worship service. Sing a hymn or two, pray, have a speaker come in and talk to players. Kind of like church. Purely voluntary."

"Gee," I said, "nothing like that has ever been done before. Do you think anybody will come?"

"One way to find out," Bobby said.

I didn't think it would catch on, but there was no harm in giving it a shot. The first-ever NBA chapel was held at Philadelphia's Spectrum Arena in February 1979, just before the 76ers played the Milwaukee Bucks. Our guest speaker was Melvin Floyd, a youth worker from urban Philadelphia. Three players showed up: Bobby, Julius Erving and Milwaukee's Kent Benson. Also present was assistant coach Chuck Daly and myself.

From that modest start, pregame chapels have spread all around the NBA. Today, every team in the league has a chapel service before each game—thanks to the bold initiative of Bobby Jones.

7. Servanthood

True leadership is about being a servant, not "the boss." The Greatest Leader Who Ever Lived took a basin and towel and stooped to wash the dirty feet of 11 true disciples and 1 traitor. In so doing, He transformed the world. Leaders lead by serving and serve by leading. You can't lead if you won't serve.

Edwin Louis Cole, author of *Strong Men in Tough Times*, put it this way: "You can only lead to the degree you are willing to serve. . . . The more you serve, the greater you become. Many people today consider the status of a servant to be demeaning, but in God's kingdom, instead of being appointed to lead, we are anointed to serve."[5]

Jesus taught His followers by word and example that servanthood, not "bosshood," is the true path to greatness: "Whoever wants to become

---

Leaders lead by serving and serve by leading.
You can't lead if you won't serve.

great among you must be your servant" (Matt. 20:26). We call ourselves followers of Christ—but do we really practice the servant-leadership He modeled? As Christian leaders, do we serve others by encouraging them to unleash their creativity—or do we just give orders? Do we serve by elevating and empowering others—or do we just use people to advance our own careers? Are we servant-leaders—or just bosses?

I recently attended a leadership training session at the Billy Graham Training Center at The Cove in Asheville, North Carolina. There I talked with Cliff Barrows, who has been the music director for the Billy Graham crusades for some 60 years. I asked him how he would describe Dr. Graham as a leader. He said, "Dr. Graham is a servant-leader because he has an enlarged heart—a big heart for people. With Billy it's never about power and prestige. It's always about others."

Herb Kelleher is former president and CEO of Southwestern Airlines. *Fortune* magazine once recognized him as "perhaps the best CEO in America" for running an airline that was consistently tops in its field for on-time performance, customer satisfaction and profitability. "I have always believed that the best leader is the best server," says Kelleher. "And if you're a servant, by definition, you're not controlling."

SERVANT-LEADERSHIP IN THE HOME

Servant-leadership is not only the key to successful leadership in business and in the church—it's also the key to leadership in the home. As Christian fathers, following the example of Asher, we are called to serve our families. This means that we regularly pray for our wife and our kids, blessing them and asking God to meet their deepest needs. It means that we study the Word of God regularly and then speak God's Word to our family every day.

I recently had Terry Meeuwsen as a guest on my Orlando radio show. Terry is cohost of *The 700 Club* and a former Miss America. She told me, "One day I interviewed Billy Graham and I asked him, 'If you could go back and change anything in your life, what would it be?' Dr. Graham replied, 'I'd do less ribbon-cutting and store openings, and spend more time with the Lord in His Word.'" Hearing that, I thought,

Wow! If Billy Graham feels that way, what about my priorities? No question, one of the most important ways we can serve our families is by spending time with God, reading His Word.

Another effective (and much neglected) way to be a servant-leader in the home is by serving our wives. When you do acts of service for your wife, you not only meet her needs but you also set a powerful leadership example for your kids. Remember what the apostle Paul said:

> Husbands, love your wives, just as Christ loved the church and gave himself up for her. . . . Husbands ought to love their wives as their own bodies. He who loves his wife loves himself (Eph. 5:25,28).

When you serve your wife, you show your children how the Lord Jesus sacrificed Himself to serve us—and how we should, in turn, serve others. Here are some practical ways to serve your wife.

Take the initiative to study the Bible and pray with her every day. Initiate outings in the park or walks in the neighborhood—just to be together and enjoy each other's company. Talk to her, ask her how she's feeling, ask her if there's anything you can do for her. Take her out to dinner, to a play or a movie, to a mountain or beach retreat. Turn off the TV and just talk to her and listen to her—no agenda, no distractions.

Offer to help your wife with grocery shopping. Fix breakfast on the weekends or give her an evening off by offering to barbecue. Stay with the kids so she can go out with friends for a few hours or a whole weekend. Do chores around the house without being asked. Treat her like a lady—stand when she enters the room, open doors for her, help her with her chair and her coat. Compliment her hair or her dress.

Eugene Peterson's paraphrase of Paul's teaching on marriage puts the whole issue of serving our wives into a fresh new perspective:

> Husbands, go all out in your love for your wives, exactly as Christ did for the church—a love marked by giving, not getting. Christ's love makes the church whole. His words evoke her beauty.

Everything he does and says is designed to bring the best out of her, dressing her in dazzling white silk, radiant with holiness. And that is how husbands ought to love their wives. They're really doing themselves a favor—since they're already "one" in marriage (Eph. 5:25-28, *THE MESSAGE*).

As Paul makes clear, Jesus is our example of servant-leadership in every arena of our lives—in the office, the church and the home:

Your attitude should be the same as that of Christ Jesus: Who, being in very nature God, did not consider equality with God something to be grasped, but made himself nothing, taking the very nature of a servant, being made in human likeness (Phil. 2:5-7).

Larry Burkett, the late founder of Crown Financial Ministries, once said, "Most families drift for lack of a rudder—the father's leadership. If a family's most important need is a godly father, and it is, then this need is far more important than all the material possessions a parent can provide." What does it mean to be the spiritual leader in the home? To me, spiritual leadership means two things: first, praying *for* my family; and second, praying *with* my family. I believe that if a Christian father does not demonstrate spiritual leadership in these two areas, he deprives his family of spiritual nurture and endangers his family by leaving his wife and children exposed to the enemy's attack.

God has entrusted your wife and children to your care. You are the steward and guardian of their welfare and safety. As Christians, we are engaged in a war—a spiritual war. This is not a metaphor. It's real warfare, and the enemy wants to turn you and your family into real casualties of that war. As the spiritual leader in your home, you have a strategic role to play. Your assignment is to pray for your family and with your family. Your goal is to lead your family to a deeper relationship with Jesus Christ.

God expects leaders to pray for the ones they lead. A leader who does not pray is failing in his leadership responsibility before God. In fact, a leader who does not pray is committing a *sin* against God. We see this principle in the words of the prophet Samuel: "As for me, far be it from me that I should sin against the LORD by failing to pray for you. And I will teach you the way that is good and right" (1 Sam. 12:23).

We sometimes forget that life—including family life—is a battlefield. We forget that the enemy is out to destroy us any way he can. As Peter reminds us, "Be self-controlled and alert. Your enemy the devil prowls around like a roaring lion looking for someone to devour" (1 Pet. 5:8). What loving father would let a lion attack his precious family? Protect your family from the enemy through the power of prayer.

HOW TO PRAY *FOR* YOUR FAMILY

Here are some ways you can pray more effectively for your family.

Build a Habit of Praying Daily for Your Family

Let's be candid: If you don't already pray daily, a new habit of prayer is hard to build. So here's a suggestion: Find another Christian dad who wants to build this habit into his life, and then you can mutually support each other in a daily discipline of prayer. Read your Bible and keep a journal of spiritual insights during your daily prayer times. Write down your prayer requests—and record the date that they are answered. Commit yourself to this discipline for at least a month and you'll build a habit that's hard to break.

Pray Specifically

As you become aware of specific needs in the lives of your wife and children, ask God to provide what each person needs. Above all, remember that each member of your family is targeted for attack by the enemy, so ask God to guard each one from physical harm, temptation, lust, peer pressure, worldly pressure, doubt and other spiritual and moral dangers.

Pray for Yourself

Ask God to mold and shape you into the man He wants you to be. Ask Him for the strength and grace to serve as a good role model and an example of Christian character. Ask Him to help you reflect God's perfect and heavenly fatherhood through your own earthly fatherhood.

Pray through the Lord's Prayer, Matthew 6:9-13.

How to Pray *with* Your Family

Praying *for* your family is only half the battle. The other half of the battle is to pray *with* your family. God commanded fathers to be spiritual leaders in the home when He said:

> Hear, O Israel: The LORD our God, the LORD is one. Love the LORD your God with all your heart and with all your soul and with all your strength. These commandments that I give you today are to be upon your hearts. Impress them on your children. Talk about them when you sit at home and when you walk along the road, when you lie down and when you get up (Deut. 6:4-7).

God calls each of us, as Christian dads, to teach His truth to our families, to pray with them, and to lead them in daily worship of the Lord. We're mistaken if we think that worship only happens in church. God intended for worship to be the centerpiece of family life.

It takes initiative and self-discipline to be a spiritual leader in the family. It means you have to set a time when the TV is switched off, the homework stops, the phone goes unanswered, and the family gathers together for a devotional time. Some Christian families like to make this a nightly ritual before bedtime. Others like to have family devotions after the evening meal, when everyone is already gathered around the table. Other families like to have devotions around the breakfast table before the day's work begins. Don't say, "I'm too busy" or "My family's schedule is too hectic." If you and your family are too busy for family devotions, you're too busy, period.

Some families call the devotional time the "family altar." This term refers to Bible times when a father, as head of the household, would lit-

We're mistaken if we think that worship only happens in church. God intended for worship to be the centerpiece of family life.

erally build an altar of stones where he and his family would worship God. For example, we read that Noah "built an altar to the LORD and, taking some of all the clean animals and clean birds, he sacrificed burnt offerings on it" (Gen. 8:20). And we read that Abram (who was later called Abraham) came to a place called Bethel "where he had first built an altar. There Abram called on the name of the LORD" (Gen. 13:4).

Today we don't need a literal altar of stone to worship God. Wherever your family gathers for worship is your altar. Here are some suggestions for building a family-altar tradition in your home.

Begin with Scripture Reading

The passage doesn't have to be long. In fact, it's a good idea to be sensitive to short attention spans. Sometimes you and your family may find real depth of meaning in a few short verses. Choose a version of the Bible that's easy for everyone to understand. As the spiritual leader, you may want to do most of the Bible reading, though it's good for kids to gain experience reading God's Word aloud.

Take a Few Minutes to Talk Together About the Passage

Facilitate discussion, but don't monopolize it. Avoid embarrassing your kids if they give an answer that seems "wrong" to you. Find a way to affirm their ideas and their sincerity, and then build on what they say in order to bring out the deep truths of the passage.

Share Thanksgiving and Prayer Requests

Take a minute or two and let each family member express a one-sentence statement of gratitude to God ("I'm thankful to God for . . .") and a brief prayer request. Encourage your kids to share prayer requests about their fears, conflicts and problems. Take each request seriously, and make sure every request is prayed for.

Pray Around the Circle

Let each family member pray out loud. Prayers need not be long. Again, be sensitive to short attention spans.

Pray for Needs Outside the Immediate Family

Demonstrate the importance of interceding in prayer for others—for relatives, friends, neighbors, missionaries, the church, people in need, people who are sick, and people who need to know the Lord. Pray, too, for our government leaders, our nation, our soldiers, our world. Pray for Christians undergoing persecution. When sharing prayer requests about the needs of others, make sure that your "requests" don't deteriorate into gossip or criticism of others. You want to lift others up in prayer—not tear them down.

Avoid Boredom

Don't let your family altar become a dry and tortuous ritual. Show enthusiasm and energy at all times. Find ways to vary the experience and keep it interesting. Show a brief video that illustrates a Scripture passage. Use pictures, maps and object lessons. Get out your guitar and lead your family in singing worship songs. Don't let the time drag; keep it short and sweet and exciting. Make sure your kids know that it's pleasant to be in the presence of the Lord.

Memorize Scripture Together

Learn a new Scripture passage together every week. Use an easy-to-understand Bible version (if you were raised on the *King James Version*, you may have to relearn the verses). Teach your kids to memorize a phrase at a time. Use flash cards to help them fix the verse in their minds. Give plenty of encouragement and affirmation when they recite the verses correctly. Here are some suggested passages to memorize:

> Have I not commanded you? Be strong and courageous. Do not be terrified; do not be discouraged, for the LORD your God will be with you wherever you go (Josh. 1:9).

> The LORD is my shepherd, I shall not be in want. He makes me lie down in green pastures, he leads me beside quiet waters, he restores my soul. He guides me in paths of righteousness for his name's sake. Even though I walk through the valley of the shadow

of death, I will fear no evil, for you are with me; your rod and your staff, they comfort me. You prepare a table before me in the presence of my enemies. You anoint my head with oil; my cup overflows. Surely goodness and love will follow me all the days of my life, and I will dwell in the house of the Lord forever (Ps. 23).

Trust in the LORD with all your heart and lean not on your own understanding; in all your ways acknowledge him, and he will make your paths straight (Prov. 3:5-6).

But those who hope in the LORD will renew their strength. They will soar on wings like eagles; they will run and not grow weary, they will walk and not be faint (Isa. 40:31).

Ask and it will be given to you; seek and you will find; knock and the door will be opened to you (Matt. 7:7).

For God so loved the world that he gave his one and only Son, that whoever believes in him shall not perish but have eternal life (John 3:16).

Jesus said to her, "I am the resurrection and the life. He who believes in me will live, even though he dies (John 11:25).

Jesus answered, "I am the way and the truth and the life. No one comes to the Father except through me" (John 14:6).

For all have sinned and fall short of the glory of God (Rom. 3:23).

For the wages of sin is death, but the gift of God is eternal life in Christ Jesus our Lord (Rom. 6:23).

Love is patient, love is kind. It does not envy, it does not boast, it is not proud. It is not rude, it is not self-seeking, it is not easily angered, it keeps no record of wrongs. Love does not delight in evil but rejoices with the truth. It always protects, always trusts, always hopes, always perseveres. Love never fails (1 Cor. 13:4-8).

But the fruit of the Spirit is love, joy, peace, patience, kindness, goodness, faithfulness, gentleness and self-control. Against such things there is no law (Gal. 5:22-23).

For it is by grace you have been saved, through faith—and this not from yourselves, it is the gift of God—not by works, so that no one can boast (Eph. 2:8-9).

Be kind and compassionate to one another, forgiving each other, just as in Christ God forgave you (Eph. 4:32).

Cast all your anxiety on him because he cares for you (1 Pet. 5:7).

If we confess our sins, he is faithful and just and will forgive us our sins and purify us from all unrighteousness (1 John 1:9).

Here I am! I stand at the door and knock. If anyone hears my voice and opens the door, I will come in and eat with him, and he with me (Rev. 3:20).

Also, have your kids memorize the order of the books of the Bible so that they can always turn to any passage without fumbling or peeking at the contents page.

LEAD YOUR CHILDREN TO CHRIST

Oh, and don't forget your Number One responsibility as the spiritual leader in your home: *Lead your children to Christ!* How do you do this? Read Bible stories to them. Teach them to pray. Answer their questions about God and the Bible. And above all, invite them to pray with you to receive Jesus Christ as Lord and Savior of their lives. I hope you've had that experience, my friend. I hope you know the joy of explaining the plan of salvation to your children and praying a simple prayer with them—a prayer like this one:

Heavenly Father,
I thank You for loving me and having a plan for my life. I've sinned
so many times. Lord, I'm sorry for my sins, and right now I want
to turn away from my sin and I want to live for You. I invite
Jesus into my life as Lord and Savior.
Thank You for hearing and answering my prayer. Please seal this decision
I've made and help me live every minute of the rest of my life for You!
Thank You in Jesus' name. Amen.

In February 2005, Dr. James Dobson spoke at the chapel service for the NBA All-Star Weekend in Denver. He gave a challenging message and closed by telling the story of how in the winter of 1988 he invited NBA legend Pete Maravich to give his Christian testimony on the Focus on the Family radio show. Pete came to know Jesus Christ as his Lord and Savior in 1982, and Dr. Dobson was looking forward to interviewing him on the show.

Before the scheduled taping, Dobson invited Pete to a gym in Pasadena for a pick-up game of basketball. After they had played for about 45 minutes, Dr. Dobson said, "Pete, you can't give up this game! You're too good!"

"I haven't played in almost a year," Maravich said. "I haven't felt good lately. I've had these chest pains."

"How do you feel today?"

"I feel great!" Pete said. Those were his last words.

Dr. Dobson started to walk away—then he heard Pete crash to the floor. Dr. Dobson and another man applied CPR while someone called for an ambulance. But Pete Maravich was already gone, dead at the age of 40. An autopsy later revealed a previously undetected heart defect, an unconnected left coronary artery. Pete had died wearing a printed T-shirt that read "Looking Unto Jesus."

That evening, Dr. Dobson went home and broke the news of Pete's death to his teenage son, Ryan. Then he said, "Ryan, one day you're going to get the same news about me. I won't be here forever. It's just a matter of time until I go to the same place Pete went today. And I just have one thing to tell you: Be there. I'm going to heaven, Ryan, and I want you to be there, too."

I had the job of giving the closing prayer after Dr. Dobson's message. It took me two full minutes to gain my composure. I want the same thing for all my kids that Dr. Dobson wants for his son. I want my kids to be there. Someday I'll be in heaven with the Lord, and I want all of my kids there with me.

There's no joy in the world like knowing that your kids will be with you in eternity. And there's no more crucial leadership task you have than leading your children to Christ.

Notes

1. Pat Williams with Jim Denny, *The Magic of Teamwork: Proven Principles for Building a Winning Team* (Nashville, TN: Thomas Nelson Publishers, 1997).
2. Pat Williams, *The Paradox of Power: A Transforming View of Leadership* (New York: Warner Faith, 2002).
3. Andy Stanley, *Visioneering: God's Blueprint for Developing and Maintaining Personal Vision* (Sisters, OR: Multnomah Publishers, 2001).
4. John Baldoni, *Personal Leadership: Taking Control of your Work Life* (Rochester, MI: Elsewhere Press, 2001).
5. Edwin Louis Cole, *Strong Men in Tough Times* (Southlake, TX: Watercolor Books, 2002).

Raise a Generation of Outstanding Leaders

Our first glimpse of our two Korean-born daughters was in June 1983, when we received a 3x5 black-and-white photo of a pair of toddlers. Their faces were dirty and their hair looked as if it had been trimmed by a buzz saw. Neither girl was smiling. They'd gotten their start in life by being left on the front steps of a police station in Seoul. The names on their I.D. tags were Yoo Jung and Yoo Jin, but we named them Andrea Michelle and Sarah Elizabeth.

The girls arrived in Philadelphia on Wednesday, September 23, 1983, after a 27-hour flight on Northwest Airlines. Andrea, age two, and Sarah, age three, were carried off the plane by an off-duty flight attendant who served as the girls' escort. I instantly felt that same surge of incredible joy I had felt when my birth children were born. We had arrived at the airport as a family of five; we went home a family of seven. That's how our family was introduced to the miracle of adoption—a miracle we would experience again and again in years to come.

We applied for another pair of kids from Korea. At the urging of Jimmy and Bobby, we requested boys this time. By this time, we were living in Orlando, where I was working on building a new NBA franchise, the Orlando Magic. On May 1, 1987, our family gathered at the Orlando airport to greet two new five-year-old brothers, Sang Wan and Sang Hyung, whom we renamed Stephen and Thomas. Arriving home, Stephen and Thomas stopped at the front door, removed their shoes, and set them neatly beside the door. We thought, *What a great idea!*

The next thing we knew, we *all* took our shoes off and lined them up beside the door. Thus began a Williams family tradition. From then on, whenever any Williams kids entered the house, they had to take their shoes off—not only to honor the traditions of our two newest brothers, but also to save wear and tear on our carpets!

We learned of four Filipino brothers, ages four to nine, who were wards of the court. Taking them in would expand our brood from eight to twelve. It would mean adding rooms to the house, buying more bunk beds, purchasing another van—and just think of the college tuition! But when we saw the photo of those four boys in front of the orphanage, smiling broadly despite their hardships, our hearts melted. David, Peter, Brian and Samuel joined our family in November 1988.

In two Romanian orphanages—one in the little Carpathian mountain village of Sibu and the other in downtown Bucharest—we found two little girls who captivated our hearts. Gabriela and Katarina joined our family in 1991, bringing our total to 14.

In the summer of 1992, we visited the slums and orphanages of São Paulo and Rio de Janeiro in Brazil. It was my first trip to the Third World, and it was a real eye-opener. Everywhere we went, I saw kids and I'd say, "Let's adopt that one! And that one! And that one!" It tore my heart out that I couldn't take them all home.

In the end, we adopted an 11-year-old girl, Rita Gomez, who had grown up in the streets of São Paulo, and an 11-year-old boy, Anderson D'Oliviera. We renamed the boy Richie after my friend Rich DeVos, and Rita chose her own new name, Daniela (Dani for short). They joined our family on February 22, 1993, bringing the total number of Williams kids to 16.

At the same time that Richie and Dani joined our clan, we heard about a brother and sister in Brazil whose father was dead and whose mother was in prison—so two more Brazilian kids joined our family. We named the eight-year-old boy Alan and the ten-year-old girl Caroline. We brought them home on Christmas night 1993.

Six months after Caroline joined our family, I was sitting with her and several of our other kids, watching the movie *Annie*. After the movie ended and the other kids ran outside to swim, Caroline stayed behind and began to cry. I said, "Why are you crying, sweetheart?"

She wrapped her arms around me and said, "I'm so happy I've got a daddy!"

Well, we *both* had tears in our eyes! As if that wasn't enough to melt my heart, she also wrote me a letter around the same time:

Dear Dad,

I'm doing very good at school, and I'm almost doing good at swiming. I'm really geting good at school. I remember when I got here and I didn't know a single word in inglesh. Because of you and mom I already know now to speak inglesh. Thank you for puting me in Killarney Elementry and for puting me in E.S.O.I. class.

I do remember when you went to brazil and pick me and alan to u.s.a. Because of you dad, I have now a knew life and knew famlly and my brothers & sisters. Now me and alan is not thos peoples from street that begs from door to door for food.

Dad I want to say thank you for all the things you did for me. God bless you and keep you for ever. In whatever you do.

Thanks again for everything, dad.

Love you daddie,

Caroline

Wow! I still get chills when I read that! And you know what? I got hugs, kisses, I-love-yous, and notes like this one from all my kids the whole time they were growing up! The psalmist wrote, "Sons are a heritage from the LORD, children a reward from him" (Ps. 127:3)—and who knows the truth of those words better than a guy with 19 kids? To this day, when people ask me how many kids I have, I say, "Nineteen, including 14 adopted—but I forget which 14!"

NEVER TOO YOUNG TO LEAD

If we want to raise a generation of leaders in the Asher tradition, we need to start today. Any kid can be a leader if given the opportunity. Every child should get a chance to lead the class or Scout troop, to lead in family devotions, to be the captain of the team.

After Donovan McNabb's rookie year with the Philadelphia Eagles (1999), he started the Donovan McNabb Foundation, a charitable organization that funds diabetes research. Donovan has also served as the national spokesman for the American Diabetes Association.

Donovan invited me to be the principle speaker for the foundation's inaugural dinner in June 2000 at Chicago's Hyatt Regency Hotel. It was a Saturday night I'll long remember. I sat at the table with Donovan, his fiancée, his parents and his brother Sean. He had grown up in the Chicago area, and you could tell at a glance that the McNabbs were a unique family. That evening, I had a chance to converse at length with Donovan McNabb and his family, and I could tell that Sam and Wilma McNabb had done a fine job of raising Donovan to be an outstanding leader.

"My parents have always been big supporters for me, and have always been kind of my number one critics," Donovan once said. "They were the ones who made sure I stayed humble. They have always been there to let me know that I needed to set a good example, because kids are watching. It matters what we say and what we do. We're role models, first and foremost, so we need to make sure we're doing the right things."

Sam McNabb agrees. "I taught both my children, 'Let your actions speak,'" he once told an interviewer. "There's a strong scripture in Proverbs that says if you train a child in the proper direction, when he grows older he will not depart. Donovan's handled some situations better than I would have. I'm proud to see his growth and development as a man. I'm proud he lets his actions represent him. Words don't always communicate effectively. Actions take care of any uncertainty." Asher himself couldn't have said it any better!

In the 1938 film *The Adventures of Robin Hood*, there's a scene in which Robin, played by Errol Flynn, arrives in Sherwood Forest. The Merry Men approach him and one of them says, "Robin Hood! You've come to join us!" To which Robin Hood replies, "No, I have come to lead you."

Everything rises and falls on leadership—it always has and it always will. John Quincy Adams, the sixth president of the United States, put it this way: "If your actions inspire others to dream more, learn more, do more and become more, you are a leader."

Vince Lombardi, the great Green Bay Packers coach of the 1960s, was a superb leader. Every Thursday morning before practice, Coach Lombardi would ask his players, "Who's going to lead today?" That's a good question for us all: Who's going to lead today? More important, who's going to lead tomorrow?

Kids *want* to lead. They enjoy setting goals and then taking the steps to achieve those goals. When do kids become bored? When they feel they are being forced to do something they don't care about. When do they rebel? When they feel they are being told what to do and how to do it. But give them a chance to lead, give them the opportunity and responsibility to make their own decisions, and they will astonish you with their ability to get things done.

In 2 Chronicles 34:1-2, there's a great statement about one of Israel's most wise and godly rulers: "Josiah was eight years old when he became king, and he reigned in Jerusalem thirty-one years. He did what was right in the eyes of the LORD and walked in the ways of his father David, not turning aside to the right or to the left." That is not a typo, my friend. Josiah was *eight years old* when he began to rule over Israel—and the Scriptures speak more highly of this young leader than of almost any other king in Israel's history! The rest of 2 Chronicles 34 is the fascinating story of this young king's reign, and the chapter ends with these words in verse 33: "As long as [Josiah] lived, [the people of Israel] did not fail to follow the LORD, the God

> When you give kids a chance to lead and the opportunity and responsibility to make their own decisions, they will astonish you with their ability to get things done.

of their fathers." So don't tell me that kids can't be leaders!

What do kids need from us in order to lead? Mostly, they just need confidence. They need to hear us say, "I believe in you, and I'm behind you all the way. You call the shots; you make the decisions—but if you need any help or support, just say the word and I'll be there for you."

As your kids learn and grow in their leadership ability, become a cheer-leader. Make a big deal over little achievements. Downplay mistakes and failures. Focus on growth and confidence-building, not perfection. Treat every failure not as a defeat but as an opportunity for learning lessons and achieving future success.

I love watching kids discover their own leadership ability. Each child is unique. Each approaches the task of leadership in his or her own way. I have watched kids accept leadership roles in the home, in church youth groups, in youth sports teams and in many other settings, and it's end-lessly fascinating to see each kid discover a leadership style to match his or her own unique personality.

Let's look again at the seven dimensions of leadership:

1. Vision
2. Communication
3. People Skills
4. Good Character
5. Competence
6. Boldness
7. Servanthood

Each of these skills or traits can be taught. None of these compo-nents of leadership is beyond the reach of a child or adolescent. Your kids can grow in each of these seven dimensions of godly leadership. Here are some ways we can build these seven leadership dimensions into our children's lives.

1. Vision

One of our jobs as parents is to encourage our kids to dream big dreams—huge, daunting, Mount Everest-sized dreams! Sometimes we parents make the mistake of trying to let a little of the air out of our kids' dreams. We're afraid that if their dreams are too big, they'll be disappointed when their dreams don't come true. I think we shortchange our kids when we try to shield them from big dreams.

My dad made that mistake when I was in high school. He was a great encourager and a wonderful father in every way—except on this one occasion. He knew that I dreamed of being a big league ballplayer, and I think he worried that my dreams would be dashed one day. Like many parents, he probably thought I should have "something to fall back on" in case my dreams didn't come true. So, out of a clear blue sky, he said, "You know, Pat, you're never going to play in the big leagues."

I was crushed. He saw it on my face and tried to make up for it.

"Look, Pat, you know I believe in you," he added. "You're going to do great things someday. I just don't want you to be disappointed if you don't make it to the big leagues."

Well, if I didn't make it into the big leagues, I was going to be disappointed—but so what? Life is full of disappointments. Character is made from disappointments. We should never pull the dreams out from under our kids. If a kid shoots for the moon, he may only get over the fence—but what of it? Let him aim high. In fact, help him aim higher! If he shoots for the moon, tell him, "Raise your sights toward Mars!" If he shoots for Mars, tell him, "Aim for the next galaxy!" Help your kids dream big dreams and see amazing visions.

Condoleezza Rice is the first African-American woman to serve as U.S. Secretary of State. She was raised in Birmingham, Alabama, during times of racial unrest. She recalls that her parents, John and Angelena Rice, had a master plan for her life. They wanted to expose her to everything good the world had to offer, while protecting her from the bigotry of segregated society. "My parents were very strategic," she told the *Washington Post*. "I was going to be so well prepared, and I was going to do all of these things that were revered in white society so well, that I would be armored somehow from racism. I would be able to confront white society on its own terms."[1]

Angelena Rice taught Condi to play piano at age three. John Rice taught Condi how to run football plays from the time she was four. Dad and daughter often sat together in front of their black-and-white TV watching Cleveland Browns games. But her parents couldn't always shield her from the effects of race hatred. In September 1963, Condi's 11-year-old friend Denise McNair was one of four girls killed in the infamous bombing of the Sixteenth Street Baptist Church.

Though Condoleezza grew up in a segregated society, her parents taught her to accept no limits on her dreams. As she put it, "My parents had me absolutely convinced that, 'Well, you may not be able to have a hamburger at Woolworth's, but you can be president of the United States!'"[2]

So encourage your kids to dream big dreams and tackle impossible challenges. If your child dreams of harpooning a great white whale, say, "I know you can do it—and I'll bring the tartar sauce!"

2. Communication

A leader must be a communicator. The ability to communicate is often the catalyst that transforms an aimless young person into a motivated young leader.

Senator George McGovern, the Democratic nominee for president in 1972, discovered his leadership ability through public speaking. "My high school English teacher told me I had a talent, both in literary expression and in speaking," Senator McGovern told me. "She introduced me to the high school debate coach, who transformed me from a somewhat shy and reticent student into a more confident and persuasive public speaker." In college, young McGovern was elected class president and won a statewide speaking competition with a talk called "My Brother's Keeper." Only when he saw himself as a speaker did he realize he was also a leader.

When young people master the ability to speak in public, their confidence level soars. Confidence gained in one area of life carries over to

The ability to communicate is often the catalyst that transforms an aimless young person into a motivated young leader.

all others. The confidence to communicate is the confidence to lead. Here are some tips to share with young people to help them become more confident communicators:

- *Be prepared.* Have your material so well organized and well practiced that you can deliver it in your sleep.
- *Keep it simple.* Limit your talk to three main points. Tell an opening story to get your audience's attention, and then tell your audience your three main points. Let your audience know where you're going. At the end, restate your three main points so that the audience knows where you've been. When you keep it simple, you make it memorable.
- *Keep it conversational.* Speak from a few simple notes—don't read a script. In your notes, use trigger words and symbols to jog your memory. Don't deliver an oration; have a conversation with the audience.
- *Tell stories.* Nothing rivets the attention or illustrates a principle better than a good story. Whenever I speak to an audience, I watch to see if people start checking their watches. If their attention drifts, I can always get it back by saying, "Let me tell you a story . . ."
- *Practice.* Give your talk again and again. Practice giving it different ways. Don't memorize! Instead, make sure your talk sounds new, fresh and conversational every time you give it.
- *Move.* If possible, walk around the stage, or even move out into the audience. Use big gestures to make a point. Use your hands when you talk—and never put them in front of you in the "fig-leaf" position (that makes you look nervous). Make eye contact with individuals in the audience. Be energetic, be enthusiastic and smile!
- *Don't worry about mistakes.* If you lose your place, just pause, take a sip of water, or tell a story. Don't be afraid that people will judge you for a goof or two. Odds are, they won't even notice.

I give around 150 speeches a year, and I keep these 7 principles in mind every time I speak. If your kids will follow these simple rules, they will quickly build the confidence to communicate in public—and to lead.

3. People Skills

Leaders need people skills. They need to know how to make a good impression, how to listen and speak, how to motivate others, how to resolve conflicts, and how to give affirmation and praise. The better our kids' people skills, the more influence they will have for Jesus Christ. Here are some of the basic people skills you should teach your kids:

- Always enter a room with confidence and purpose.
- Greet people with a firm handshake and a warm smile.
- Stand straight and look people in the eye.
- Speak in a strong, clear voice.
- Use these words freely and often: "Please." "Thank you." "I don't know, but I'll find out." "My mistake. It won't happen again." "I'm sorry. Please forgive me."
- Listen before speaking. Don't interrupt.
- Accept compliments graciously without becoming conceited.
- Accept criticism without defensiveness or anger.
- Give frequent compliments, affirmation and praise—and say it in front of the whole team.
- Offer criticism gently and in private.
- Keep confidences. Don't gossip. (Even if it's "true," it's still gossip.)
- Don't spread yourself too thin. Learn to say no politely but firmly.
- Be a good human being. Treat others as you want to be treated.

Oh, and here are a few more bits of advice you should give your kids: Never say or do anything out of anger. Donate blood every year. Leave generous tips. Give cheerfully to your church and other charities. Don't just give money, but give time as well. (I don't know if this last paragraph is really about people skills, but it's good advice anyway!)

4. Good Character

People admire and follow choice men and choice women of proven character. We need to teach young leaders to build strong, positive character traits into their lives: honesty, integrity, humility, a strong work ethic, responsibility, self-discipline, courage, kindness, fairness, tolerance, and so forth.

In the Scriptures, we clearly see that God views character as an integral part of an authentic leader. In Psalm 78, we read:

> [The Lord] chose David his servant
> and took him from the sheep pens;
> from tending the sheep he brought him
> to be the shepherd of his people Jacob,
> of Israel his inheritance.
> And David shepherded them
> with integrity of heart;
> with skillful hands he led them (vv. 70-72).

Here we catch a glimpse of how God chose a young shepherd boy and trained him to be a leader. David needed to learn to shepherd sheep before he could shepherd a nation. His sheep-tending days were days of leadership preparation. And what was God looking for in a shepherd of His people? Integrity of heart. In a word, *character*.

5. Competence

The leadership dimension of competence is a combination of several factors: a competitive spirit, training, experience, the ability to delegate responsibility to others, and a commitment to excellence. How do you build competence in a young leader? Here are some tips:

- *Teach diligence.* Make sure your child knows that work comes before play. TV, video games and other forms of amusement are not an entitlement; they are a reward *after* their work is done—and done *well*. Make sure they know that if a job hasn't been done with diligence and excellence, it isn't done, period. And if it isn't done, it will have to be done again and again until it *is* done.

- *Teach responsibility.* Each kid should have a set of chores (posted on the fridge or the family corkboard) for which he or she is responsible. No one in the family should be reminded a dozen times to do a given chore; the child is responsible to do it without being told. Responsible behavior is rewarded; irresponsible behavior is penalized. Teach kids to be self-starters and to get work done without being nagged.

- *Teach respect for authority.* Kids should be told that there is no arguing or disrespect allowed, period. Sure, you're willing to listen when they raise an issue in a reasonable and respectful fashion. But the moment a child treats you with disrespect, the discussion is over and consequences ensue. Be sure to handle the matter calmly. Avoid disciplining in anger.

- *Teach your kids a healthy attitude toward work.* The Bible teaches us that work is a gift from God. Solomon wisely wrote, "That everyone may eat and drink, and find satisfaction in all his toil—this is the gift of God" (Eccles. 3:13). And Paul tells us, "Whatever you do, work at it with all your heart, as working for the Lord, not for men" (Col. 3:23).

- *Let your children see you at work.* Take your kids to the office when you can. Let them help you with the yard work and other chores. Involve them in big family work projects like home remodeling or landscaping so that they can see you at work and experience with you the satisfaction of a job well done. Mentor them and help them acquire the work skills you learned from your parents and mentors.

- *Teach your children about money.* When you give your kids their allowance, encourage them to set aside at least 20 percent—10 percent (minimum) as a tithe to the Lord and another 10 percent for savings. Teach them to avoid the pitfalls of materialism, consumerism and debt. Help your kids to become competent managers of their money. Teach them about investing—and especially about "the miracle of compounding." Show them that if they invest early and allow their money to earn interest year after year, they will earn interest on the principle—and on the interest.

- *Invest in your kids' competence.* If you want to raise competent young leaders, you need to give your children opportunities to increase their competence—and that's not cheap. You may have to buy musical instruments or sports equipment; you may have to attend Little League games or dance recitals. The kids who achieve competence in any endeavor are those whose parents were willing to sacrifice a lot of time and a lot of money.

Bob Feller was a 16-year-old Iowa farm boy when he was signed to pitch for the Cleveland Indians in 1935. In his rookie season with Cleveland, he won 17 games; the next year, 24 games. He went on to pitch for Cleveland for 18 years, winning 266 games and losing 162. His career was interrupted by a 4-year hitch in the Navy, where he became a highly decorated anti-aircraft gunner aboard the U.S.S. *Alabama.* Baseball historians believe that had he not been interrupted at the height of his career, he could have recorded 350 wins and 3,500 strikeouts.

Feller credits his dad with giving him the opportunity to develop his skills at an early age. "My father never played ball," Feller once recalled, "but he had great dreams for me. I don't think he ever doubted that I'd eventually play professional ball. We played baseball together while I was growing up. He pitched batting practice to me and even built me a batting cage out of leftover lumber and chicken wire. . . . He bought me proper equipment, too—a uniform, spikes, a good glove always, and official league balls.

"Probably the greatest thing he did for me was when I was twelve and we built a complete ball field on our farm. We called it Oakview, because it was up a hill overlooking the Raccoon River and it had a beautiful view of a grove of oak trees. We had a complete diamond with an outfield fence and scoreboard and even a grandstand behind first base. We charged a small admission to cover our expenses. My father transported the players and my mother fed them. . . . We drew some pretty fair-sized crowds on certain weekends. I was the only real 'kid' on our team, but I did just fine. Oakview Park was my incubator as a pitcher. Looking back on it now, I have to be pretty thankful that my father was the man he was."

What sacrifices are you willing to make to build the competence of your young leader? How much are you willing to spend? How much time are you willing to invest?

6. Boldness

You can't be a leader without boldness. As General Omar Bradley once said, "Act boldly and unseen forces will come to your aid." To become leaders, your kids will have to overcome shyness, fear and the desire to play it safe. As parents, teachers, coaches and mentors, we need to push our kids out of their comfort zones. We have to help them gain the confidence and the spirit of adventure that every true leader needs. Here's a game plan for nurturing the boldness and courage of your young leader:

- *Encourage your young leader to research the risks.* A good leader is daring but never reckless. He takes risks—but only *calculated* risks. Good leaders tilt the odds in their favor by being informed and leaving as little as possible to chance.
- *Teach your young leader how to organize and plan.* Sloppiness and poor preparation should never be mistaken for boldness. Strategic planning is the key to victory in any bold venture.
- *Encourage your young leader to be boldly decisive.* Motivational speaker Brian Tracy put it this way: "Decisiveness is a characteristic of high-performing men and women. Almost any decision is better than no decision at all." And the inimitable Yogi Berra put it even more succinctly: "When you come to a fork in the road, take it."
- *Build optimism.* Leaders must have an optimistic confidence in

To become leaders, your kids will have to overcome shyness, fear and the desire to play it safe. We need to push our kids out of their comfort zones.

God, in themselves and in their ideas and decisions. Optimism is contagious; it spreads from leaders to followers, lifting the entire team.

- *Accept failure as a lesson, not a defeat.* The downside of risk-taking is obvious: Sometimes you lose. But so what? Failure may well be the best teacher your young leader will ever have. He'll get through it—and he probably won't make the same mistake again.

Walt Disney was 21 years old when he founded his first animation company, Laugh-o-Gram Films. One year later, he went bankrupt. When he was in his late twenties, an unscrupulous distributor stole his most popular cartoon character from him—so Walt created a plucky little mouse named Mickey, and the rest is history. If Walt had not had a few failures early on, he would never have invented Mickey Mouse. He later observed, "It's important to have a good hard failure when you're young. I learned a lot out of that. . . . I've never been afraid."

Courage and confidence are necessary ingredients in the makeup of every warrior and every leader. As John C. Maxwell puts it, "Leaders must take others into the unknown and march them off the map." We can't very well tell our kids, "Dream big dreams—but play it safe! Don't take chances!" No, we have to tell them, "Reach for your dreams! Act boldly and make your dreams come true!"

7. Servanthood

We need to raise up a generation of young leaders who understand that they are not here to intimidate, dominate and oppress people; they are here to *serve* people. Authentic leadership, based on the example of Jesus, is not about being the boss but about being a servant.

On June 28, 2005, I attended the 25th Anniversary Gala of the Washington Speakers Bureau, the most prestigious agency in the country. Many of the agency's top speakers were there, including Rudy Giuliani, Lou Holtz, Tom Peters, Tom Ridge, Joe Theissman and Colin Powell. Near the end of the dessert reception, I saw that General Powell and his wife were about to leave. I introduced myself and told him that my 28-year-old son Bobby is a baseball manager in the Washington Nationals farm system. General Powell is a partner in a group trying to buy the team.

"General Powell," I said, "what advice would you give my son as he starts his managerial career?"

Without hesitating, General Powell said, "Tell your son these three things: First, take care of your troops. Second, keep your mouth shut and do your job every day. Third, don't worry about your next job." With that, he turned and went off into the night. Those are three powerful insights into what it means to be a leader—and the first of those insights—"take care of your troops"—is a call to servanthood. A leader takes care of his troops.

My friend Gil McGregor, announcer and color commentator for the New Orleans Hornets, taught me a concept he calls The Dirty Shoulders Principle. "Servants always have dirty shoulders," he told me. "They're always lifting people up and letting them stand tall on their own shoulders. A servant doesn't care who gets the glory. He just lifts others up."

I recently visited Coach John Wooden at his home in Southern California. Coach Wooden is "the Wizard of Westwood," the legendary coach of the UCLA Bruins from 1948 to 1975. As I walked into Coach's home, I found myself in a museum of memorabilia from his long career in college sports. But the most fascinating section of Coach Wooden's personal museum was an area of his front hallway that was devoted to two people who had nothing to do with sports: Abraham Lincoln and Mother Teresa.

"Tell me, Coach," I said, "why have you devoted this portion of your home to Abe Lincoln and Mother Teresa?"

"They're my heroes," he said. "I admire them because they were servants. They had such wonderful character qualities—courage, integrity, humility, self-sacrifice, all the things that make a great servant. Can you think of two better heroes to have than Lincoln and Mother Teresa?"

I couldn't. Coach Wooden had chosen as his heroes two people who were among the greatest leaders the world has ever known—and not coincidentally, two of the greatest servants.

So the next time a young person asks you how to become a leader, just say, "If you want to be a leader, be a servant! Find a lawn that needs mowing and mow it—for free. Find a house that needs painting and paint it. Clean your room, load the dishwasher, set the table, wash the car. If you see a mess, clean it up—even if it's not your mess. Pull weeds in your neighbor's flowerbed. Go to the homeless shelter and make sandwiches or ladle soup. Go to Starbucks or a rock show and share your faith with someone. If you want to be a leader, be a servant."

In his book *The Legacy: Ten Core Values Every Father Must Leave His Child*, Steven J. Lawson tells the story of a little girl who always looked up to her father, who was an artist. As he stood at his easel, brushing oil paints onto large canvases, she'd be on the floor at his feet, coloring in her coloring book.

Occasionally, the father would lift her onto his lap, place one of his brushes in her tiny hand and then gently guide her hand. Together, father and daughter would dip the brush in the paint and then apply the colors to the canvas. In the process, this child developed a love for painting.

Years passed. The child became a teenager. One summer day in 1967, she was swimming near the Magothy River on Chesapeake Bay. She took a dive off a boat, not realizing that the water was too shallow for diving. She hit the bottom and broke her neck.

Though paralyzed from the neck down, today she is an artist like her father. Her name is Joni Eareckson Tada, and she paints by holding the paintbrush in her mouth. Her paintings and books are a ministry of God's grace in millions of lives. Joni is a Christian servant-leader and a spiritual descendent of Asher. Her father mentored her and gave her the gift of artistic expression—a gift that could not be taken away even by a paralyzing accident.[3]

That's the task God sets before each of us as fathers, grandfathers, coaches, teachers and mentors: We are to grasp the hands of these young leaders and gently but firmly guide them toward lives of purpose, meaning, leadership and servanthood. If we do our part, God will do His. He will lead them down the path to a future of service and servanthood.

If we build a generation of leaders who are spiritual descendents of Asher, God will use them in a mighty way. They will be an unstoppable force for good in the world. God will make sure that nothing keeps them from becoming all He has called them to be.

DO THE MATH

I sometimes wonder if Asher had this whole thing planned out. Did he deliberately set out to raise up thousands of descendents to be fathers, men of character, warriors and leaders? Or was it all just a natural consequence of the kind of man Asher was and the way he lived his life?

I don't know. The Scriptures don't tell us. But I do know this: You and I can *choose* to be like Asher. We can strategically and deliberately implement the Asher principles and *choose* to become men of influence, warriors who shape the destiny of generations to come.

As a father of 19 kids, I have given this a lot of thought. Do you realize how many grandchildren I could have someday? The average family has 2.3 children. Just do the math and you'll find that I can expect to have 43.7 grandkids. And what if my kids were to exceed the averages and have 4, 5 or 6 kids per family? What if they all caught the adoption bug and (gasp!) had 8 kids? Or 12? Or—?

Whoa! Don't even go there! I just had a mental picture of some future Williams family Thanksgiving—with a cast of thousands!

When we started adopting, I never sat down with a financial planner and counted the cost. I just took the plunge. Where did this fire in my soul come from—this mania to adopt kids from around the world? The truth is, I don't know. All I can say is that I would look at some dog-eared photo from the Philippines or I'd walk through an orphanage in Brazil and I just couldn't help myself. I seemed to feel God nudging me in the ribs and saying, "Pat, these are My kids. Help them! Take them in!" (And you know how persuasive *He* can be!)

To tell you the truth, I can't go to orphanages anymore. I'm like a

If we build a generation of leaders who are spiritual descendents of Asher, God will use them in a mighty way. They will be an unstoppable force for good in the world.

recovering alcoholic who can never walk past a tavern. I can't trust myself with that kind of temptation. I can't afford to adopt any more kids. So what do I do instead? I spread the word.

Let me give it to you straight: Adoption isn't easy and it isn't cheap. Sure, there are a lot of warm fuzzies when you bring that kid into your life. But there are also some hard realities. Most of these kids come from rough backgrounds. Some are street kids. They've seen a lot and they've been knocked around by life. Don't expect them to fit right in. Don't expect them to instantly adapt to a new language, a new culture, and new family rules. There'll be tantrums, fears, crying, sleepless nights, bedwetting, and more.

Do the hugs, smooches, smiles, I-love-you-daddys, cute faces, and warm fuzzies make up for all the hassle and expense? Absolutely! And I'll even throw in the teenage years when I say that! It's all been worth it. And the best part is knowing that these children are growing up to be people of Christlike character. They'll have families; they'll be choice men and women; they'll be leaders; they'll be warriors in the cause of Christ.

After Caroline had been with us less than a year, I took her to a playground near our home. I watched her while she was on the swings. Nearby were a little boy and his parents. I struck up a conversation with them and found out that they were Orlando Magic fans and knew who I was.

"Do you have other children?" the woman asked.

I laughed. "Do I have other children!" I told her *exactly* how many children I had—and the woman turned pale!

"We just have two boys," she said, "and we can't have any more kids, so we've been thinking about adopting a little girl. Problem is, they put us on a waiting list and it takes years to get a child. We're afraid that when we're finally approved, we'll be too old to be parents anymore!"

"Well, you're looking in the wrong country."

"The wrong country?"

"Absolutely. There's a shortage of adoptable kids in America. But if you go to other countries, especially in the developing world, there are thousands of kids with no one to adopt them. We found Caroline in Brazil."

I didn't think Caroline was listening, but just then she piped up and said, "And those little girls need mommies and daddies, too!" And she's absolutely right.

Every chance I get, I talk about adoption, especially international adoption. Every day, I pray that more people will catch this dream in which all of God's children, no matter where they come from in the world, will have daddies and mommies. I pray that Christian families will take these kids in, give them a home, and tell them about a heavenly Father who loves them.

Is God nudging you in the ribs right now? I'm not asking you to adopt 14 kids—but could you take 1 or 2? Could you think about it? Pray about it? That's all I'm asking.

THE FINAL PRINCIPLE

In the spring of 1855, a Sunday School teacher named Edward Kimball entered Holton's Shoe Store in Boston. He went to a young shoe clerk and said, "Young man, I want you to know that Jesus loves you." They talked for a few minutes and the clerk got down on his knees and asked Jesus Christ to take control of his life. The clerk's name was Dwight L. Moody.

Moody became a world-renowned evangelist. In 1879, he held a series of meetings in England. In the audience was a disillusioned and defeated pastor named F. B. Meyer. When Meyer heard Moody speak, he surrendered his life to Jesus Christ—and he became one of the great evangelical preachers of his day.

One man who heard F. B. Meyer preach was J. Wilbur Chapman. So impressed was Chapman that he became an evangelist like Meyer. He founded an organization combining Christianity with athletics, the Young Men's Christian Association (YMCA).

Through the YMCA, Chapman mentored a young baseball star. The player, Billy Sunday, shook up the sports world by quitting baseball to become an evangelist. When Billy Sunday preached a series of evangelistic meetings in Charlotte, North Carolina, some Charlotte businessmen were so moved that they organized a committee to bring more evangelists to town. One of the preachers they invited was Mordecai Ham from Kentucky.

In 1934, during one of Mordecai Ham's revival meetings, a troubled young man listened to the message and struggled with God. At the end of the service, the young man went forward and invited Jesus Christ to be Lord of his life. That young man's name was Billy Graham.

How many people has Dr. Billy Graham preached to during his years of ministry? No one knows, but the number is certainly well over a billion or two. And we can trace Dr. Graham's lifetime of ministry back to a Sunday School teacher who said to a Boston shoe clerk, "I want you to know that Jesus Christ loves you."

When you decide to have an influence on one young life, you never know the chain of events you might set in motion. Roll a little snowball down a mountainside and you just might start an avalanche!

Let's say that you're an average dad in an average family and that you have an average number of kids—2.3 children. Okay, that three-tenths of a kid bothers me, too, so let's round it off to 2 kids. Now let's say you adopt 2 more. That's 4. While you're raising your own 4 kids, you also decide to become a Sunday School teacher, a Scoutmaster, or a coach. Now you're mentoring and influencing dozens of kids!

And you know, I'll bet there are some kids in your church who don't have a dad. Think of the impact you could have by taking those kids to a ballgame or on a camping trip with your family. Maybe there are some kids in your neighborhood who have never heard that Jesus loves them. Maybe you could tell them about Jesus while you're driving them to Sunday School.

Asher had thousands of descendents—not just physical descendents but spiritual descendents: heads of families, choice men, brave warriors and outstanding leaders. You and I can have the same kind of impact on the world. Not only can we leave behind a generation of physical descendents to carry on our family name, but we can also leave behind a generation of spiritual descendents to carry on the name of Jesus Christ.

Children are a blessing from the Lord. The more children we influence for Him, the more blessing God pours out upon the world. So here is the last and most important of all the Asher principles: *The man who blesses a child blesses the world.*

Friend, I urge you: Be that man—that gentle, godly warrior. Bless that child. Change the world.

Notes
   1. Dale Russakoff, "Lessons of Might and Right: How Segregation and an Indomitable Family Shaped National Security Adviser Condoleezza Rice," *The Washington Post*, September 9, 2001; page W23. http://www.washingtonpost.com/wp-dyn/articles/A54664-2001Sep6.html (accessed November 2005).
   2. "Profile: Condoleezza Rice," *BBC News World Edition*, January 20, 2005. http://news.bbc.co.uk/2/hi/americas/3609327.stm (accessed November 2005).
   3. Steven J. Lawson, *The Legacy: Ten Core Values Every Father Must Leave His Child* (Sisters, OR: Multnomah Press, 1998).

IMAGINE A LEGACY . . .

Asher was old. His hair and beard were white. He lay on a mat in a house far from where he was born. There were people all around the room. They had come to be close to him because they loved him.

The four sons of Asher—Imnah, Ishvah, Ishvi and Beriah—were there. They were all gray-bearded grandfathers now.

Asher's daughter, Serah, was near to him, too. Although her face was netted with fine lines, she was still graceful and slender, and her eyes were wide, brown and clear, like the eyes of a doe.

Only Ijona was missing. Asher's wife had preceded him in death.

Asher's eyesight had darkened with age, but he could still recognize the faces of his sons and grandsons who had become heads of families, choice men, brave warriors and outstanding leaders. They made him proud. He rejoiced to see how large and fine his family had become. He could die at peace, knowing that his family walked with God.

Asher felt a tug at his sleeve. It was his little great-granddaughter, Shua. "Great-grandfather," she said, "are you going to die now?"

Mortified, Shua's mother whispered, "Shua! You mustn't ask that!"

Asher chuckled. "Why not?" he said. "It's a good question." Then, to the little girl, he said, "Yes, Shua, I'm going to die now."

Shua thought it over, and then asked, "Does it hurt to die?"

"No, child," Asher said, "it doesn't hurt. I just feel very, very tired."

Shua's older brother, Japhlet, crowded close to Asher's bedside. Tears brimmed in the boy's eyes. "I don't want you to die, Great-grandfather."

"It's all right," Asher said, weakly patting the boy's arm. "I've lived a long time and learned many things. I have taught those things to your grandfather, and your grandfather has taught them to your father, and your father will teach them to you. So when your father speaks, listen to him."

"I will, Great-grandfather," Japhlet said, wiping his eyes.

"Good," Asher said. "And someday you will teach those things to your own sons, won't you?"

"Yes, Great-grandfather. I promise."

"I know you will." Asher settled back onto his deathbed. He seemed to grow weaker by the moment. "Serah? Are you there, my daughter?" His eyes were open but unseeing.

"I'm here, Father."

Asher smiled. "Serah," he said, "do you remember that song you used to sing in the vineyard when you'd bring water to your brothers and me?"

"I remember," Serah said.

"I'd like to hear that song again."

Serah sang, "There is no one holy like the Lord, there is no one besides You! There is no Rock like our God!" Her voice quavered as she sang, but Asher didn't seem to notice. His eyes slowly closed. His lips smiled faintly.

When Serah finished singing, she placed her hand on her father's chest and leaned down to kiss him. The moment her lips brushed his cheek, she knew: Her father had gone to be with the Lord he loved.

Asher's journey on Earth was done.

The Asher Movement

At the beginning of this book, I told you how I was introduced to Asher by Pastor Cal Rychener of Northwoods Community Church in Peoria, Illinois. As my work on this book was drawing to a close, I called Cal and told him about *The Warrior Within*. I said, "When you told me about that little verse in 1 Chronicles, you had no idea what you triggered in my life! My journey with Asher has been a thrill ride!"

He said, "Oh, I know what you mean! Asher has certainly affected lives here in Peoria."

"I believe it," I said. "Could you tell me one of those stories?"

"Certainly," said Cal, and he proceeded to tell me about a young man he's become acquainted with, one of his daughter's coworkers. The man's name is Ruben, and when Cal met him, he was not attending any church.

One Friday night in October 2004, Cal went to a Barnes and Noble bookstore. He noticed Ruben and his wife sitting at a table, immersed in a stack of business books, so he went over to say hello.

Cal was wearing a T-shirt with large type across the front that read, simply, "7:40." Seeing Cal's shirt, Ruben said, "What does '7:40' mean?"

"That stands for our Seven-Forty Club. It's a men's group that meets on the first Saturday morning of every month. We have breakfast, Bible study and prayer together. We're meeting tomorrow morning, in fact."

"That sounds like something I need," Ruben said. "Could I come?"

Cal noticed that Ruben's wife wiped away tears as she said, "Ruben, you really need to go to that."

Ruben showed up the next morning promptly at 7:40. The men had a great time of fellowship and Cal gave them a message from the Bible. Afterwards, Ruben came to Cal with tears rolling down his cheeks. He was thumping his chest with the flat of his hand, as if there was an intense struggle going on in Ruben's heart.

"Pastor Cal," Ruben said, "I need to talk to you. Could I call you this week?"

They set up a time. Later that week, they had a long talk about the intense soul-searching Ruben was going through. Cal invited Ruben to church, and the next Sunday, Ruben and his wife were sitting right up front.

Cal was preaching a series of evangelistic messages. As a visual aid, he'd had a bridge built on the stage. The bridge had steps at either end, but there was a large piece missing out of the middle—a gap so wide that no one could walk across. That gap represented the gulf of sin between God and humanity.

Yet, there was a way for the gap to be bridged. As Cal talked about the cross of Christ, a wooden cross was placed in that gap. Now anyone could cross the bridge by simply walking over on the cross.

Cal looked out over the audience and called people forward. The people he called got out of their seats, went up on the stage, and walked across the bridge by means of the cross. Cal invited anyone who wanted to make a decision for Christ to join that procession and step across the bridge. Many people made that life-changing decision.

After the service was over, Ruben stayed behind in the sanctuary, looking at that bridge, thinking about what it meant. When he and Pastor Cal were alone, Ruben said, "Pastor, I want to walk across the bridge. Would you walk it with me?"

So the two men went up on the stage and walked across the bridge by means of the cross. When they walked down the steps on the other side, Ruben said, "Pastor, would you pray with me?"

The two men got down on their knees, and Ruben prayed to receive Jesus Christ as his Lord and Savior.

Three weeks later, Ruben's wife came to Pastor Cal after a Sunday morning service. "I always thought I was a Christian," she said, "but as I've listened to you explain what it means to have Jesus as the Lord of your life, I realize I'm not really a Christian. I want to walk across the bridge. Will you walk with me like you did with Ruben?"

So Pastor Cal crossed the bridge and prayed with her, too.

As Cal finished telling me that story, he said, "Ruben and his wife are two of the most excited, glowing, committed Christians I've ever met."

"And you know what's amazing?" I said. "God used something as simple as your '7:40' T-shirt to trigger a transformation in their lives. If you hadn't worn that shirt, Ruben wouldn't have asked about the meaning of 7:40."

"God is doing things like that all the time," Cal said. "Ever since our church discovered Asher, this thing has been snowballing and taking on the shape of a real movement!"

"Well, Cal," I said, "the Asher movement has certainly swept me up! I'm ready to take this message to every church in America!"

The Asher principles have transformed my life, as well as my speaking and writing ministry. As I look around at the problems in American society, the American family and the American church, I can't help but think that so many problems could be solved if we men would make a commitment to become spiritual descendents of Asher—heads of Christian families, choice men of Christian character, brave Christian warriors, and outstanding Christian leaders. Our world would be transformed if we would become the warriors God created us to be—complete in all four dimensions of godly manhood.

Will you make that commitment with me? Will you choose to become what Asher was—a complete man of God?

This generation and generations to come are waiting for your answer.

ACKNOWLEDGMENTS

With deep appreciation I acknowledge the support and guidance of the following people who helped make this book possible:

Special thanks to Bob Vander Weide and Rich DeVos of the Orlando Magic.

I'm grateful to my assistant, Diana Basch, who managed so many details that made this book possible. Thanks also to Peggy Matthews Rose for her invaluable critique of the manuscript; and to Timothy Denney, who provided wise and practical insights on prayer.

Hats off to four dependable associates—my colleague Andrew Herdliska, my adviser Ken Hussar, Vince Pileggi of the Orlando Magic mail/copy room, and my ace typist Fran Thomas.

Hearty thanks also go to Bill Greig III, Kim Bangs, Steven Lawson and Mark Weising of Regal Publishing Group, and to my partner in writing this book, Jim Denney. Thank you for believing we had something important to share and for providing the support and the forum to say it.

And finally, special thanks and appreciation go to my wife, Ruth, and to my wonderful and supportive family. They are truly the backbone of my life.

—Pat Williams

YOU CAN CONTACT PAT WILLIAMS AT:

Pat Williams
c/o Orlando Magic
8701 Maitland Summit Boulevard
Orlando, FL 32810
Phone (407) 916-2404
pwilliams@orlandomagic.com
www.patwilliamsmotivate.com

If you would like to set up a speaking engagement for Pat Williams, please write his assistant, Diana Connery, at the above address or call her at (407) 916-2454. Requests can be faxed to (407) 916-2986 or e-mailed to dconnery@orlandomagic.com.

We would love to hear from you. Please send your comments about this book to Pat Williams at the above address or in care of our publisher at the address below. Thank you.

Pat Williams
c/o Regal Publishing Group
1957 Eastman Ave.
Ventura, California 93003

God's Word for Your World

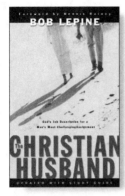

The Christian Husband
God's Job Description for a Man's
Most Challenging Assignment
Bob Lepine
ISBN 08307.36891

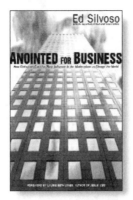

Anointed for Business
How Christians Can Use Their
Influence in the Marketplace
to Change the World
Ed Silvoso
ISBN 08307.41968

Living Life Boldly
No Regrets, No What-Ifs—
Selling Out to What Really Matters
Ted Roberts
ISBN 08307.31083

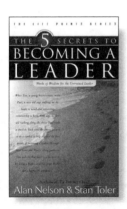

**The Five Secrets to
Becoming a Leader**
Words of Wisdom for
the Untrained Leader
Alan Nelson and Stan Toler
ISBN 08307.29151

**Moments Together
for Couples**
Daily Devotions for Drawing Near to
God and One Another
Dennis and Barbara Rainey
ISBN 08307.17544

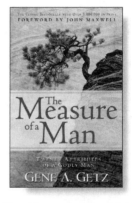

The Measure of a Man
Twenty Attributes of a Godly Man
Gene A. Getz
ISBN 08307.34953

Go One-on-One with Sports Legends

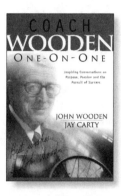

**Coach Wooden
One-on-One**
Inspiring Conversations on
Purpose, Passion and the
Pursuit of Success
John Wooden and *Jay Carty*
ISBN 08307.32918

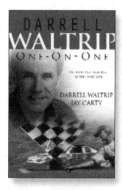

**Darrell Waltrip
One-on-One**
The Faith That Took Him
to the Finish Line
Darrell Waltrip and *Jay Carty*
ISBN 08307.34635

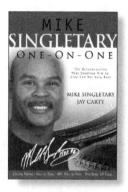

**Mike Singletary
One-on-One**
The Determination That Inspired
Him to Give God His Very Best
Mike Singletary and *Jay Carty*
ISBN 08307.37022

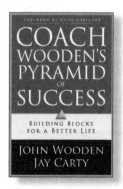

**Coach Wooden's
Pyramid of Success**
Building Blocks for a Better Life
John Wooden and *Jay Carty*
ISBN 08307.36794

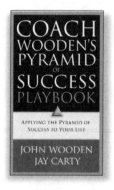

**Coach Wooden's Pyramid
of Success Playbook**
Applying the Pyramid of Success to
Your Life
John Wooden and *Jay Carty*
ISBN 08307.37936